R. Giusti

SIGNATURES

Discovering Courage

Senior Authors

Roger C. Farr

Dorothy S. Strickland

Authors

Richard F. Abrahamson ♦ Alma Flor Ada ♦ Barbara Bowen Coulter

Bernice E. Cullinan ♦ Margaret A. Gallego

W. Dorsey Hammond

Nancy Roser ♦ Junko Yokota ♦ Hallie Kay Yopp

Senior Consultant

Asa G. Hilliard III

Consultants

V. Kanani Choy ♦ Lee Bennett Hopkins ♦ Stephen Krashen ♦ Rosalia Salinas

Harcourt Brace & Company

Orlando Atlanta Austin Boston San Francisco Chicago Dallas New York Toronto London

 ISBN 0-15-308320-4

6 7 8 9 10 048 99

Voices of the Wild
by Jonathan Lawson, illustrated by Wayne McLoughlin

A Chorus of
CULTURES

MY NAME IS
María Isabel
by Alma Flor Ada
illustrated by K. Dyble Thompson

MARY STOLZ
Storm in
the Night
illustrated by PAT CUMMINGS

LESTER'S DOG
by Karen Hesse Illustrated by Nancy Carpenter

Brave Irene
by William Steig

DISCOVERING COURAGE

CONTENTS

DISCOVERING COURAGE

How do you find courage when you need it? Can other people help you be brave? The characters in this theme find the answers to these questions. Maybe they will help you find courage, too!

DISCOVERING COURAGE

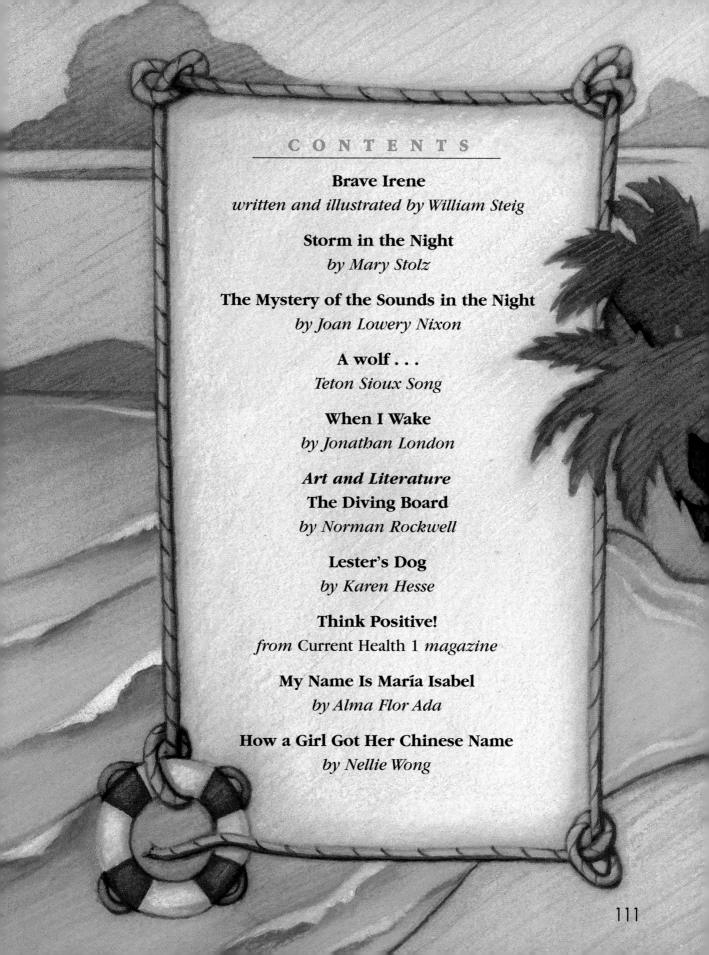

CONTENTS

BOOKSHELF

Frida María
by Deborah Nourse Lattimore

Frida finds the courage to be true to herself—the best Frida there ever was!

Award-Winning Author and Illustrator
Signatures Library

The Wave
by Margaret Hodges

One man's courage and quick thinking save an entire Japanese village from ruin.

New York Times Best Illustrated Book; Caldecott Honor

Signatures Library

by Margaret Hodges / Illustrated

Ramona the Brave
by Beverly Cleary

Ramona bravely faces new teachers, new books, a new bedroom, and a mean dog!

Children's Choice

Annie and the Old One
by Miska Miles

Annie needs true, lasting courage to face a very sad time in her life.

Newbery Honor

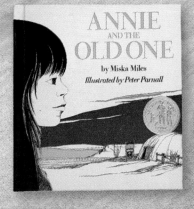

The Magic Fan
written and illustrated by Keith Baker

Yoshi finds a magic fan and saves a town from a tidal wave.

SLJ Best Books; Notable Trade Book in Social Studies

Brave

Brave Irene
by William Steig

New York
Times Best
Illustrated Book

Notable Trade
Book for the
Language Arts

Irene

by
William Steig

Mrs. Bobbin, the dressmaker, was tired and had a bad headache, but she still managed to sew the last stitches in the gown she was making.

"It's the most beautiful dress in the whole world!" said her daughter, Irene. "The duchess will love it."

"It *is* nice," her mother admitted. "But, dumpling, it's for tonight's ball, and I don't have the strength to bring it. I feel sick."

"Poor Mama," said Irene. "I can get it there!"

"No, cupcake, I can't let you," said Mrs. Bobbin. "Such a huge package, and it's such a long way to the palace. Besides, it's starting to snow."

"But I *love* snow," Irene insisted. She coaxed her mother into bed, covered her with two quilts, and added a blanket for her feet. Then she fixed her some tea with lemon and honey and put more wood in the stove.

With great care, Irene took the splendid gown down from the dummy and packed it in a big box with plenty of tissue paper.

"Dress warmly, pudding," her mother called in a weak voice, "and don't forget to button up. It's cold out there, and windy."

Irene put on her fleece-lined boots, her red hat and muffler, her heavy coat, and her mittens. She kissed her mother's hot forehead six times, then once again, made sure she was tucked in snugly, and slipped out with the big box, shutting the door firmly behind her.

It really was cold outside, very cold. The wind whirled the falling snowflakes about, this way, that way, and into Irene's squinting face. She set out on the uphill path to Farmer Bennett's sheep pasture.

By the time she got there, the snow was up to her ankles and the wind was worse. It hurried her along and made her stumble. Irene resented this; the box was problem enough. "Easy does it!" she cautioned the wind, leaning back hard against it.

By the middle of the pasture, the flakes were falling thicker. Now the wind drove Irene along so rudely she had to hop, skip, and go helter-skeltering over the knobby ground. Cold snow sifted into her boots and chilled her feet. She pushed out her lip and hurried on. This was an important errand.

When she reached Apple Road, the wind decided to put on a show. It ripped branches from trees and flung them about, swept up and scattered the fallen snow, got in front of Irene to keep her from moving ahead. Irene turned around and pressed on backwards.

"Go home!" the wind squalled. "Irene . . . go hooooooome . . ."

"I will do no such thing," she snapped. "No such thing, you wicked wind!"

"Go ho–o–ome," the wind yodeled. "GO HO–WO–WOME," it shrieked, "or else." For a short second, Irene wondered if she shouldn't heed the wind's warning. But no! *The gown had to get to the duchess!*

The wind wrestled her for the package—walloped it, twisted it, shook it, snatched at it. But Irene wouldn't yield. "It's my mother's work!" she screamed.

Then—oh, woe!—the box was wrenched from her mittened grasp and sent bumbling along in the snow. Irene went after it.

119

She pounced and took hold, but the ill-tempered wind
ripped the box open. The ball gown flounced out and went
waltzing through the powdered air with tissue-paper attendants.

Irene clung to the empty box and watched the beautiful gown
disappear.

How could anything so terribly wrong be allowed to happen? Tears froze on her lashes. Her dear mother's hard work, all those days of measuring, cutting, pinning, stitching . . . for *this*? And the poor duchess! Irene decided she would have to trudge on with just the box and explain everything in person.

She went shuffling through the snow. Would her mother understand, she wondered, that it was the wind's fault, not hers? Would the duchess be angry? The wind was howling like a wild animal.

Suddenly Irene stepped in a hole and fell over with a twisted ankle. She blamed it on the wind. "Keep quiet!" she scolded. "You've done enough damage already. You've spoiled everything! *Everything!*" The wind swallowed up her words.

She sat in the snow in great pain, afraid she wouldn't be able to go on. But she managed to get to her feet and start moving. It hurt. Home, where she longed to be, where she and her mother could be warm together, was far behind. It's got to be closer to the palace, she thought. But where any place was in all this snow, she couldn't be sure.

She plowed on, dragging furrows with her sore foot. The short winter day was almost done.

Am I still going the right way, she wondered. There was no one around to advise her. Whoever else there was in this snow-covered world was far, far away, and safe indoors—even the animals in their burrows. She went plodding on.

Soon night took over. She knew in the dark that the muffled snow was still falling—she could feel it. She was cold and alone in the middle of nowhere. Irene was lost.

She had to keep moving. She was hoping she'd come to a house, any house at all, and be taken in. She badly needed to be in someone's arms. The snow was above her knees now. She shoved her way through it, clutching the empty box.

She was asking how long a small person could keep this struggle up, when she realized it was getting lighter. There was a soft glow coming from somewhere below her.

She waded toward this glow, and soon was gazing down a long slope at a brightly lit mansion. It had to be the palace!

Irene pushed forward with all her strength and—*sloosh! thwump!*—she plunged downward and was buried. She had fallen off a little cliff. Only her hat and the box in her hands stuck out above the snow.

Even if she could call for help, no one would hear her. Her body shook. Her teeth chattered. Why not freeze to death, she thought, and let all these troubles end. Why not? She was already buried.

And never see her mother's face again? Her good mother who smelled like fresh-baked bread? In an explosion of fury, she flung her body about to free herself and was finally able to climb up on her knees and look around.

How to get down to that glittering palace? As soon as she raised the question, she had the answer.

She laid the box down and climbed aboard. But it pressed into the snow and stuck. She tried again, and this time, instead of climbing on, she leaped. The box shot forward, like a sled.

The wind raced after Irene but couldn't keep up. In a moment she would be with people again, inside where it was warm. The sled slowed and jerked to a stop on paving stones.

The time had come to break the bad news to the duchess. With the empty box clasped to her chest, Irene strode nervously toward the palace.

But then her feet stopped moving and her mouth fell open. She stared. Maybe this was impossible, yet there it was, a little way off and over to the right, hugging the trunk of a tree—the beautiful ball gown! The wind was holding it there.

"Mama!" Irene shouted. "Mama, I found it!"

She managed somehow, despite the wind's meddling, to get the gown off the tree and back in its box. And in another moment she was at the door of the palace. She knocked twice with the big brass knocker. The door opened and she burst in.

She was welcomed by cheering servants and a delirious duchess. They couldn't believe she had come over the mountain in such a storm, all by herself. She had to tell the whole story, every detail. And she did.

Then she asked to be taken right back to her sick mother. But it was out of the question, they said; the road that ran around the mountain wouldn't be cleared till morning.

"Don't fret, child," said the duchess. "Your mother is surely sleeping now. We'll get you there first thing tomorrow."

Irene was given a good dinner as she sat by the fire, the moisture steaming off her clothes. The duchess, meanwhile, got into her freshly ironed gown before the guests began arriving in their sleighs.

What a wonderful ball it was! The duchess in her new gown was like a bright star in the sky. Irene in her ordinary dress was radiant. She was swept up into dances by handsome aristocrats, who kept her feet off the floor to spare her ankle. Her mother would enjoy hearing all about it.

Early the next morning, when snow had long since ceased falling, Mrs. Bobbin woke from a good night's sleep feeling much improved. She hurried about and got a fire going in the cold stove. Then she went to look in on Irene.

But Irene's bed was empty! She ran to the window and gazed at the white landscape. No one out there. Snow powder fell from the branch of a tree.

"Where is my child?" Mrs. Bobbin cried. She whipped on her coat to go out and find her.

When she pulled the door open, a wall of drift faced her. But peering over it, she could see a horse-drawn sleigh hastening up the path. And seated on the sleigh, between two large footmen, was Irene herself, asleep but smiling.

Would you like to hear the rest?

Well, there was a bearded doctor in the back of the sleigh. And the duchess had sent Irene's mother a ginger cake with white icing, some oranges and a pineapple, and spice candy of many flavors, along with a note saying how much she cherished her gown, and what a brave and loving person Irene was.

Which, of course, Mrs. Bobbin knew. Better than the duchess.

William Steig

It's not surprising that William Steig has always loved to draw. His parents and his three brothers were artists, too.

William Steig was born in 1907 in Brooklyn, New York. When he was growing up, his older brother, Irwin, gave him his first painting lessons. William also liked to read fairy tales, legends about King Arthur, and adventure stories. His favorite book was *Pinocchio*.

William Steig has written and illustrated dozens of books for young readers. Most of his books are about animal characters, but some, like *Brave Irene*, are about children. He says, "For some reason I've never felt grown up."

RESPONSE

MAKE A CHART

Good Wind, Bad Wind

We know that wind is air moving over the Earth. We also know that the wind can help us or hurt us. Work with a group to make a chart. Show ways wind can help people and ways it can hurt people.

WRITE SENTENCES

Fun with Words

The author of "Brave Irene" uses words that help you see, feel, and hear what is happening in the story. For example, he says that the duchess was like "a bright star in the sky." Write three sentences that describe how something looks, feels, and sounds. Your sentences can be silly or serious.

CORNER

MAKE A GET-WELL CARD

Get Well Soon

The duchess was sorry to hear that Irene's mother was ill. Make a get-well card from the duchess to Mrs. Bobbin. In your card, tell Mrs. Bobbin what she should do for her fever. (You can find tips in the story.) Draw a picture on your card that will cheer up Mrs. Bobbin.

What Do You Think?

- How does Irene's mother feel at the end of the story? Why?

- Did you predict that Irene would make it to the palace? Why or why not?

- Was it a good idea for Irene to try to get to the palace by herself? Explain your answer.

133

Notable
Trade Book
in
Social Studies

MARY STOLZ
Storm in the Night

illustrated by PAT CUMMINGS

*S*torm in the night.
Thunder like mountains blowing up.
Lightning licking the navy-blue sky.
Rain streaming down the windows,
babbling in the downspouts.
And Grandfather? . . . And Thomas? . . .
And Ringo, the cat?
They were in the dark.
Except for Ringo's shining mandarin eyes
and the carrot-colored flames in the wood
stove, they were quite in the dark.
"We can't read," said Grandfather.
"We can't look at TV," said Thomas.
"Too early to go to bed," said
Grandfather.
Thomas sighed. "What will we do?"
"No help for it," said Grandfather, "I shall
have to tell you a tale of when I was a
boy."
Thomas smiled in the shadows.
It was not easy to believe that Grand-
father had once been a boy, but Thomas
believed it.
Because Grandfather said so, Thomas
believed that long, long ago, probably at
the beginning of the world, his grandfather
had been a boy.

*A*s Thomas was a boy now, and always would be.

A grandfather could be a boy, if he went back in his memory far enough; but a boy could not be a grandfather.

Ringo could not grow up to be a kangaroo, and a boy could not grow up to be an old man.

And that, said Thomas to himself, is that.

Grandfather was big and bearded.

Thomas had a chin as smooth as a peach.

Grandfather had a voice like a tuba.

Thomas's voice was like a penny whistle.

"I'm thinking," said Thomas.

"Ah," said Grandfather.

"I'm trying to think what you were like when you were my age."

"That's what I was like," said Grandfather.

"What?"

"Like someone your age."

"Did you look like me?"

"Very much like you."

"But you didn't have a beard."

"Not a sign of one."

"You were short, probably."

"Short, certainly."

"And your voice. It was like mine?"

"Exactly."

Thomas sighed. He just could not imagine it. He stopped trying.

He tried instead to decide whether to ask for a new story or an old one.

Grandfather knew more stories than a book full of stories.

Thomas hadn't heard all of them yet, because he kept asking for repeats.

As he thought about what to ask for, he listened to the sounds of the dark. Grandfather listened too.

In the house a door creaked. A faucet leaked.

Ringo scratched on his post, then on Grandfather's chair.

He scratched behind his ear, and they could hear even that.

In the stove the flames made a fluttering noise.

"That's funny," said Thomas. "I can hear better in the dark than I can when the lights are on."

"No doubt because you are just listening," said his grandfather, "and not trying to see and hear at the same time."

That made sense to Thomas, and he went on listening for sounds in the dark.

*T*here were the clocks.

The chiming clock on the mantel struck the hour of eight.

Ping, ping, ping, ping, ping, ping, ping, ping-a-ling.

The kitchen clock, very excited.

Tickticktickticktickticktickety.

There were outside sounds for the listening, too.

The bells in the Congregational church rang through the rain.

Bong, bong, bong, bong, bong, bong, bong, BONG!

Automobile tires swished on the rain-wet streets.

Horns honked and hollered.

A siren whined in the distance.

"Grandfather," said Thomas, "were there automobiles when you were a boy?"

"Were there *automobiles*!" Grandfather shouted. "How old do you think I am?"

"Well . . ." said Thomas.

"Next thing, you'll be asking if there was electricity when I was your age."

"Oh, Grandfather!" said Thomas, laughing.

After a while he said, "Was there?"

"Let's go out on the porch," said Grandfather. "There's too much silliness in here."

By the light of the lightning they made their way to the front door and out on the porch.

Ringo, who always followed Thomas, followed him and jumped to the railing. The rain, driving hard against the back of the house, was scarcely sprinkling here.

But it whooped windily through the great beech tree on the lawn, brandishing branches, tearing off twigs.

It drenched the bushes, splashed in the birdbath, clattered on the tin roof like a million tacks.

Grandfather and Thomas sat on the swing, creaking back and forth, back and forth, as thunder boomed and lightning stabbed across the sky.

Ringo's fur rose, and he turned his head from side to side, his eyes wide and wild in the flashes that lit up the night.

The air smelled peppery and gardeny and new.

"That's funny," said Thomas. "I can smell better in the dark, too."

*T*homas thought Grandfather answered, but he couldn't hear, as just then a bolt of lightning cracked into the big beech tree. It ripped off a mighty bough, which crashed to the ground.

This was too much for Ringo. He leaped onto Thomas's lap and shivered there.

"Poor boy," said Thomas. "He's frightened."

"I had a dog when I was a boy," said Grandfather. "He was so scared of storms that I had to hide under the bed with him when one came. He was afraid even to be frightened alone."

"*I'm* not afraid of *anything*," Thomas said, holding his cat close.

"Not many people can say that," said Grandfather. Then he added, "Well, I suppose anybody could *say* it."

"I'm not afraid of thunderstorms, like Ringo and your dog. What was his name?"

"Melvin."

"That's not a good name for a dog," Thomas said.

"I thought it was," Grandfather said calmly. "He was my dog."

"I like cats," said Thomas. "I want to own a *tiger*!"

"Not while you're living with me," said Grandfather.

"Okay," Thomas said. "Is there a story about Melvin?"

"There is. One very good one."

"Tell it," Thomas commanded. "Please, I mean."

"Well," said Grandfather, "when Melvin and I were pups together, I was just as afraid of storms as he was."

"No!" said Thomas.

"Yes," said Grandfather. "We can't all be brave as tigers."

"I guess not," Thomas agreed.

"So there we were, the two of us, hiding under beds whenever a storm came."

"Think of that . . ." said Thomas.

"That's what I'm doing," said Grandfather. "Anyway, the day came when Melvin was out on some errand of his own, and I was doing my homework, when all at once, with only a rumble of warning . . . *down* came the rain, *down* came the lightning, and all around and everywhere came the thunder."

149

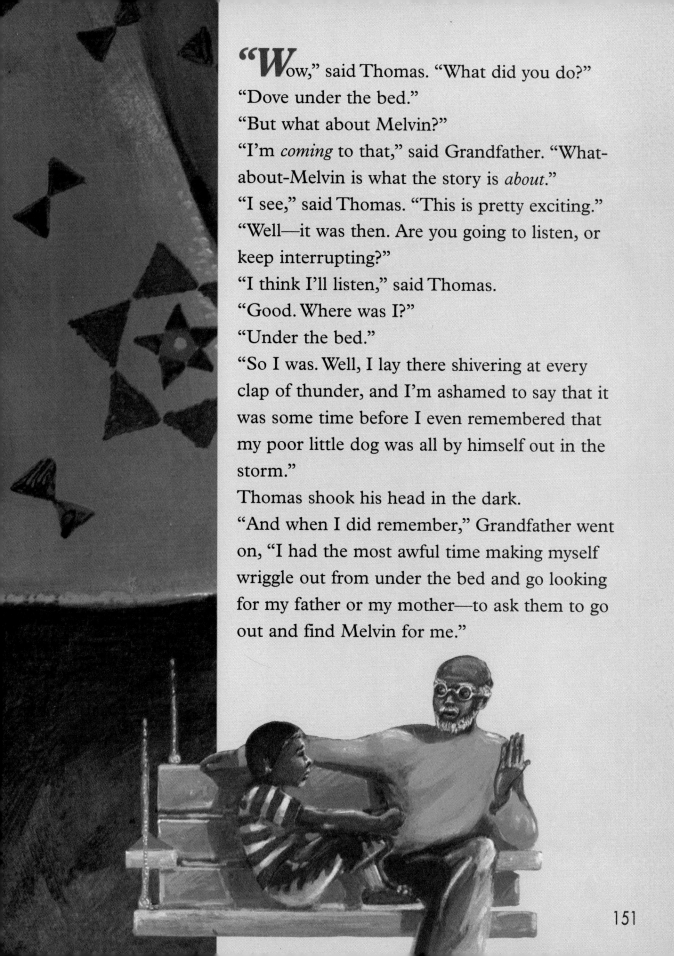

"Wow," said Thomas. "What did you do?"

"Dove under the bed."

"But what about Melvin?"

"I'm *coming* to that," said Grandfather. "What-about-Melvin is what the story is *about*."

"I see," said Thomas. "This is pretty exciting."

"Well—it was then. Are you going to listen, or keep interrupting?"

"I think I'll listen," said Thomas.

"Good. Where was I?"

"Under the bed."

"So I was. Well, I lay there shivering at every clap of thunder, and I'm ashamed to say that it was some time before I even remembered that my poor little dog was all by himself out in the storm."

Thomas shook his head in the dark.

"And when I did remember," Grandfather went on, "I had the most awful time making myself wriggle out from under the bed and go looking for my father or my mother—to ask them to go out and find Melvin for me."

"Grandfather!"

"I told you I was afraid. This is a true story you're hearing, so I have to tell the truth."

"Of course," said Thomas, admiring his grandfather for telling a truth like *that*. "Did you find them?"

"I did not. They had gone out someplace for an hour or so, but I'd forgotten. Thomas, fear does strange things to people . . . makes them forget everything but how afraid they are. You wouldn't know about that, of course."

Thomas stroked his cat and said nothing.

"In any case," Grandfather went on, "there I was, alone and afraid in the kitchen, and there was my poor little dog alone and afraid in the storm."

"What did you *do*?" Thomas demanded. "You didn't *leave* him out there, did you, Grandfather?"

"Thomas—I put on my raincoat and opened the kitchen door and stepped out on the back porch just as a flash of lightning shook the whole sky and a clap of thunder barreled down and a huge man *appeared* out of the darkness, holding Melvin in his arms!"

"Whew!"

"That man was seven feet tall and had a face like a crack in the ice."

"Grandfather! You said you were telling me a true story."

"**I**t's true, because that's how he looked. He stood there, scowling at me, and said, 'is this your dog?' and I nodded, because I w too scared to speak. 'If you don't take better care of him, you shouldn't have him at all,' sai the terrible man. He pushed Melvin at me and stormed off into the dark."

"Gee," said Thomas. "That wasn't very fair. He didn't know you were frightened too. I mean, Grandfather, how old were you?"

"Just about your age."

"Well, some people my age can get pretty frightened."

"Not you, of course."

Thomas said nothing.

"Later on," Grandfather continued, "I realized that man wasn't seven feet tall, or even terrible. He was worried about the puppy, so he didn't stop to think about me."

"Well, *I* think he should have."

"People don't always do what they should, Thomas."

"What's the end of the story?"

"Oh, just what you'd imagine," Grandfather said carelessly. "Having overcome my fear enough to forget myself and think about Melvin, I wasn't afraid of storms anymore."

"Oh, good," said Thomas.

For a while they were silent.

The storm was spent. There were only flickers of lightning, mutterings of thunder, and a little patter of rain.

155

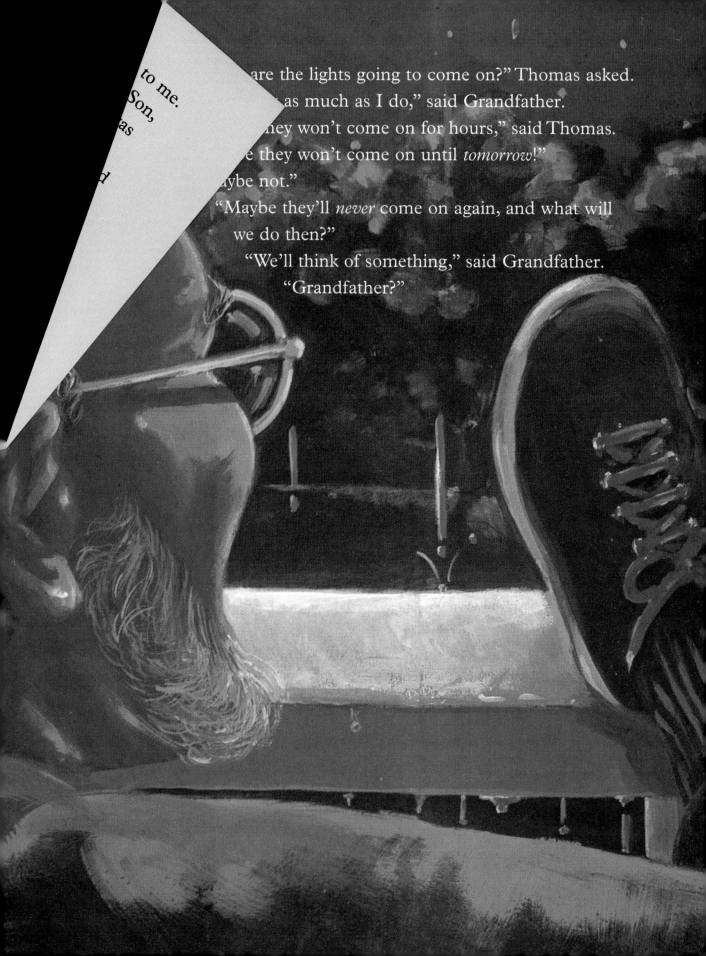

"...are the lights going to come on?" Thomas asked.

"...as much as I do," said Grandfather.

"...hey won't come on for hours," said Thomas.

"...e they won't come on until *tomorrow*!"

"...aybe not."

"Maybe they'll *never* come on again, and what will we do then?"

"We'll think of something," said Grandfather.

"Grandfather?"

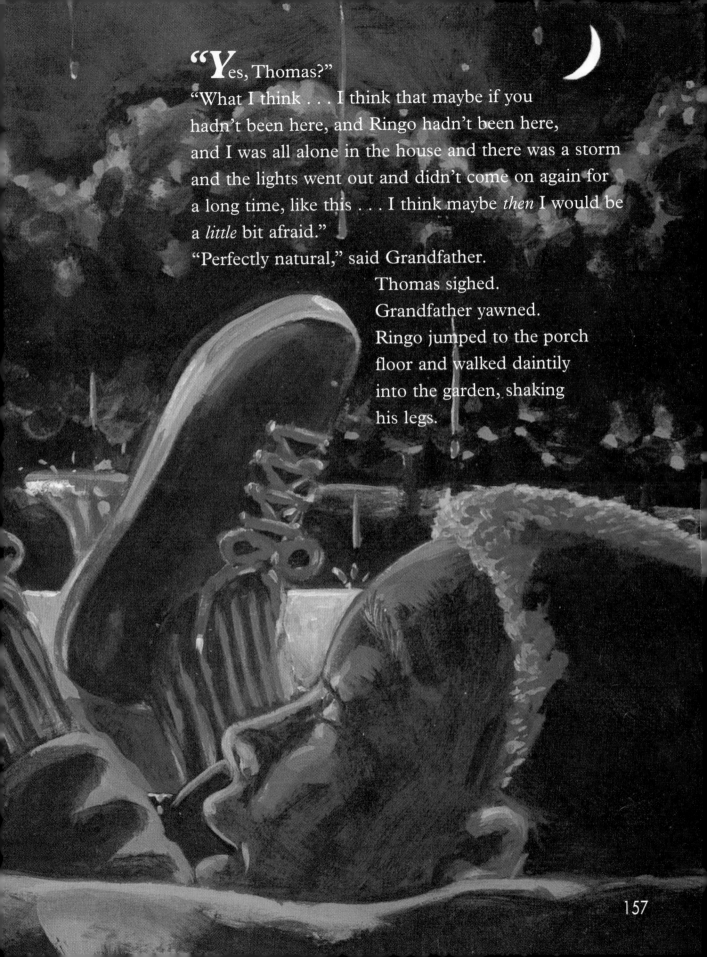

"Yes, Thomas?"

"What I think . . . I think that maybe if you
hadn't been here, and Ringo hadn't been here,
and I was all alone in the house and there was a storm
and the lights went out and didn't come on again for
a long time, like this . . . I think maybe *then* I would be
a *little* bit afraid."

"Perfectly natural," said Grandfather.

Thomas sighed.
Grandfather yawned.
Ringo jumped to the porch
floor and walked daintily
into the garden, shaking
his legs.

157

After a while the lights came on.
They turned them off and went to bed.

Meet Pat Cummings...

Writer Ilene Cooper spoke with Pat Cummings about the illustrations in this story.

Cooper: *Did you use models for the people in this book?*

Cummings: Yes. For Thomas, I used my cousin, Travis. I used a gentleman in my neighborhood named Theo for the grandfather, but I had to add a beard and mustache. Sometimes, I use my family, and I don't tell them they're in the book until it's finished. I've found that when I draw people I love and care about, the pictures feel much more real to me.

Travis was the model for Thomas.

Cooper: *What kind of paint did you use for the art in* Storm in the Night?

Cummings: Acrylic paint—it's a kind that dries very quickly. The story has a nighttime setting, so I painted the dark background first—blacks, blues, and purples. Then I added the bright parts.

Cooper: *How old were you when you started drawing?*

Cummings: I started as soon as I could hold a pencil. I always knew I was going to be an artist when I grew up.

This is an early sketch for the painting on pages 144 and 145.

Response Corner

Where Are Your Batteries?

Suppose you had no electricity for a night. What would you do? Write a plan for an evening without electricity for you and your family. Tell how you would make dinner without electricity. What could you do for an after-dinner activity? Compare your plan with a classmate's.

I'm Not Afraid...

In the beginning of the story, Thomas says that he isn't afraid of anything. Later, his grandfather teaches him an important lesson about being afraid. Write a diary entry that tells about the lesson Thomas learned.

Raining Cats and Dogs

You can get weather reports on radio and on television. You can also find them in a newspaper. Read, watch, or listen to a weather report. Then write a weather report that Thomas might have heard on the night of the storm. Describe the storm and the damage it is causing. Tell what the weather will be like for the next few days. You may want to share your weather report with your classmates.

What Do You Think?

⚡ How does Thomas feel at the end of the story? How do you know?

⚡ Do you think it's normal to be afraid of things like storms and darkness? Explain your answer.

⚡ Would Thomas and his grandfather have had such a good time if the electricity had been working? Why or why not?

161

THE MYSTERY OF THE SOUNDS

IN THE NIGHT

a play by Joan Lowery Nixon

illustrated by Cameron Wasson

CHARACTERS:

MIKE

PAUL
(his friend)

UNCLE PETE
(Mike's uncle)

TIME: *A summer evening.*

SETTING: *A clearing in the woods. On each side of stage are bushes, with twigs scattered near them. Backdrop of forest may be used.*

AT RISE: MIKE, PAUL, *and* UNCLE PETE *enter left, carrying sleeping bags.*

UNCLE PETE: Here we are, boys. This is where we'll camp for the night. It's a good thing we arrived before it got any darker.

MIKE: This is great, Uncle Pete!

UNCLE PETE (*Smiling*): Put your sleeping bags in a spot that looks comfortable. (*He puts his down at left.*)

PAUL: I can't wait to go fishing tomorrow morning! (*Looks around and puts sleeping bag down at right*)

MIKE (*Dropping sleeping bag at his feet*): I can't wait to eat dinner! When do we build the campfire?

UNCLE PETE: Right now, Mike. I'll bring the firewood,

and you two find some dry twigs to help get the fire started.

MIKE: Isn't this neat? (*Throws out his arms*) And the best part is that we can stay up as late as we want to!

UNCLE PETE: There's not much to do after dark. I think you'll want to go to sleep early.

MIKE (*Hopefully*): We could sit by the campfire and tell stories.

PAUL: I know an Indian story my grandfather once told me. It's about how brave young warriors used to go to the mountains to look for the Great Bear.

UNCLE PETE: That sounds like a good story, Paul. I can't wait to hear it. (UNCLE PETE *exits left.* PAUL *and* MIKE *collect twigs.*)

MIKE: Paul, this Great Bear in your story—just how big is he?

PAUL: He's supposed to be higher than a man . . . higher than the trees.

MIKE: That big, huh? (*He looks over his shoulder.*) It sure is quiet here in the woods, isn't it?

PAUL (*Standing still; listening*): It's almost too quiet. I can't hear a thing. (*Scratching, rustling sound is heard near bushes right.* PAUL *and* MIKE *freeze, look at each other.*) Except for something in the bushes. (*They stare at bushes.*)

MIKE: What do you think it is?

PAUL (*Nervously*): I don't know. (UNCLE PETE *reenters left, carrying firewood. He goes center and crouches, arranging wood.*)

UNCLE PETE: Where are the twigs, boys? (MIKE *and* PAUL *hurry to his side and hand him twigs.*)

MIKE: Uncle Pete, we heard scratching noises in the bushes.

UNCLE PETE: That doesn't surprise me. There are lots of animals in the woods. (*He "lights" fire and feeds twigs into it, then stands.*) There we are. The fire's going nicely now. I'll get the food out of the car.

165

PAUL and MIKE (*Ad lib*): I'll help you. Me, too. (*Etc.*)

UNCLE PETE: Thanks, anyway, but there's not that much to carry. You two stay here and keep an eye on the fire. (*He exits left. MIKE and PAUL stand very close together.*)

MIKE: I didn't think about animals being in the woods.

PAUL: Maybe they're small animals.

MIKE: *Very* small animals.

PAUL (*Holding hands close together*): Little bitty animals. (*They continue to stare at bushes. After a few moments, UNCLE PETE reenters, carrying box. He puts it down next to fire, then takes pan and ladle from box, "fills" pan, and puts it on fire.*)

UNCLE PETE: O.K., campers, you can give me a hand. Paul, why don't you stir the beans?

PAUL: Sure. (*Stirs*)

UNCLE PETE: Mike, you'll find plates and forks in the box.

MIKE: O.K., Uncle Pete.

PAUL (*Stirring*): They're beginning to bubble already.

MIKE (*Pulling plates and forks out of box*): Then let's eat!

UNCLE PETE: I'd like to hear Paul's story about the Great Bear. (*He takes ladle from PAUL and puts food onto plates. All sit at campfire, eating. UNCLE PETE is in the middle.*)

PAUL: Well, my grandfather told me that the brave young men in the tribe would go high into the mountains to see the Great Bear.

MIKE: How did they see him?

PAUL: A young man had to go into the mountains by himself. He would make a fire. He would pray to the spirits of the mountain. Then he would wait for the Great Bear.

MIKE (*Nervously*): And then what?

PAUL: If he had been a brave man, soon he would see the Great Bear. It would be higher than a man—higher than the trees.

166

MIKE (*Putting down plate, looking over shoulder, and moving closer to* UNCLE PETE): I don't think I'd like to see the Great Bear.

PAUL (*Putting down plate*): I wouldn't, either, especially when it's dark—the way it is now. (*He looks over his shoulder.*)

UNCLE PETE (*Putting down plate and standing*): I hope you boys aren't scaring yourselves. If you're afraid, you won't have a good time.

MIKE: Who's afraid?

PAUL: We're not afraid of anything.

UNCLE PETE: Good. (*He reaches into box, pulls out two flashlights, gives them to* MIKE *and* PAUL. *He takes out another flashlight for himself, and canteen.*) I should have thought about getting our drinking water before it got dark. I'm going down to the river to fill the canteen. You can spread out the sleeping bags, and I'll be back in a little while. (*Exits left*)

MIKE: Uncle Pete is right. If we're scared, we won't have any fun.

PAUL (*With false bravery*): I'm not scared. I'm not even thinking about the Great Bear! (*They both open sleeping bags, arrange them.*)

MIKE: I'm not scared, either! (*Rustling sound is heard from bushes right.* MIKE *jumps up, and shines his flashlight on bushes.*) What's that?

PAUL: I hope it's not the Great Bear! (*He hurries to stand beside* MIKE.)

MIKE (*Pointing*): Look at that! It's just a little raccoon.

PAUL (*Laughing shakily*): No one would be dumb enough to be afraid of a little raccoon.

MIKE (*Forcing laugh*): Yeah. No one. (*Rustling sound is heard from bushes left.* MIKE *and* PAUL *turn to face left.*) Did you hear that?

PAUL (*Shining his flashlight on bushes*): Aw, it's only a rabbit.

MIKE: Only a little kid would be afraid of a rabbit!

PAUL: Yeah. Just a scared little kid. (*There is cry from over their heads, off right. Boys grab each other.*) Look out! Use the flashlights!

MIKE (*Waving flashlight at spot high up, off right*): It's got eyes!

PAUL (*Stepping back, sighing*): All owls have eyes.

MIKE (*Nervously*): Is that what it is?

PAUL: Only a baby would be afraid of an owl.

MIKE: Yeah. Only a silly baby. (*Sound is heard from bushes right. MIKE and PAUL quickly turn flashlights right.*) What was that?

PAUL: Just a little mouse. See? (*Points*)

MIKE: Nobody would be afraid of a mouse.

PAUL: My mother would.

MIKE (*Sitting on sleeping bag*): Paul, we've been afraid of a lot of little animals that wouldn't hurt anybody.

PAUL (*Laughing nervously*): Pretty dumb of us, huh? (*Sits*)

MIKE: It's because we keep expecting the Great Bear to show up.

PAUL: I don't think the Great Bear would make a little noise. I think he'd make a big noise. (*Loudly*) Clump, clump, clump! (*Heavy footsteps are heard offstage. MIKE and PAUL jump up.*)

MIKE: Did you hear that? (UNCLE PETE *enters left.* MIKE *and* PAUL *look at each other, sigh with relief.*)

UNCLE PETE: What's the matter? You look as if you saw a ghost.

PAUL: Oh, nothing's the matter. You startled us, that's all.

UNCLE PETE: O.K., it's time to go to sleep. We want to get up very early and catch fish for breakfast. (*All take off their shoes and get into sleeping bags.*)

MIKE: It's really dark out here!

PAUL: Except for the stars. Look at them all, Mike!

UNCLE PETE: It's the Great Bear! (MIKE *and* PAUL *jump up, still in sleeping bags. They hop around.*)

MIKE: Where is it? Help!

PAUL (*Frantically*): Everybody run!

UNCLE PETE: Hey! Calm down! Look over our heads. Look at the stars. (MIKE *and* PAUL *stand still, look up. As* UNCLE PETE *talks, they slowly sit.*) The very bright groups of stars that you see are called "constellations." Every constellation has a name, and the one over our heads is called the "Big Dipper." Its Latin name is "Ursa Major," which means "Great Bear." Many people, including some Indian tribes, call it the "Great Bear."

MIKE: Paul, do you think that could be the Great Bear your grandfather told you about? Higher than a man, higher than the trees?

PAUL: Maybe it is.

MIKE (*Lying back*): And we were afraid of that?

PAUL (*Lying back*): Who was afraid? *I* wasn't.

UNCLE PETE: Go to sleep, boys. (*There is silence for a few moments, then a rumbling sound is heard.*)

PAUL (*Startled*): What's that?

MIKE (*Laughing*): I know what that sound is. It's Uncle Pete. That's the way he snores.

PAUL (*Laughing*): We're even scared of snoring! We're not really very brave, are we, Mike?

MIKE: We must be brave. We saw the Great Bear, didn't we? Just as the warriors did in your story.

PAUL: That's right. We're pretty brave, after all. (*He lies down.*) Good night, big warrior.

MIKE (*Lying back*): Good night, brave chief. (UNCLE PETE *continues to snore, as curtains close.*)

The End

A *TETON SIOUX* SONG
illustrated by John Clapp

A WOLF...

A WOLF
I CONSIDERED MYSELF,
BUT
THE OWLS ARE HOOTING
AND
THE NIGHT I FEAR.

WHEN I WAKE

by Jonathan London
illustrated by David Diaz

When I wake in the dark

easy on the earth

and see the shape of an owl
among the stars

I lift my voice to the silence

and give thanks

to the wild night.

175

ART & LITERATURE

What do you think Irene and Thomas would tell the boy in this picture? Would it take more courage to jump or to climb back down the ladder? Why do you think so?

The Diving Board (1947)
by Norman Rockwell

Norman Rockwell painted pictures for magazines. He became famous for his *Saturday Evening Post* covers. Rockwell's paintings show everyday life in a way that often makes people smile.

Curtis Publishing/Estate of Norman Rockwell

177

LES

LESTER'S DOG

by Karen Hesse   illustrated by Nancy Carpenter

TER'S
DOG

by Karen Hesse
illustrated by Nancy Carpenter

On long summer days,
Mama scoots me out of the house
after dinner. Same as always, I sit
on the front stoop, watching robins
rake the grass for worms, and wait
for Corey to come out.

An old Chevy slides around the corner and, gears grinding, climbs up the hill. Just before the car drops down the back side of Garrison Avenue, Lester's dog tears out from under his porch and lunges at the car's wheels. You can hear him barking clear to the end of the block. He swaggers back when the car is gone and hunkers down under his porch again. I shiver, touching the scar on my nose where Lester's dog bit me when I was six.

I'm busy wishing bad things on Lester's dog when Corey comes up beside me, sticks out his hand, and pulls me off the stoop. He's tugging like he wants me to follow him up the hill, to the top of Garrison Avenue.

I shake my head. "I'm not going past Lester's dog tonight," I say. But Corey's bigger than I am, and he steers me up the hill anyway. It doesn't matter what you say to Corey, 'cause he can't hear you, and even if he could, he's too stubborn to listen.

We pass Corey's house first, and then Mr. Frank's. I sort of count on Mr. Frank always being there, sitting in his big chair, looking out over the block. Mama says he's a broken man since Mrs. Frank died, and I've been wondering for some time now just what it'd take to fix him.

I wave to him and he nods back. That's our way of talking, me and Mr. Frank.

We're almost at Lester's house now, its lawn all patched and dusty, and the grass gone from Lester's dog digging it up. I'm so scared of that dog the hair's standing up on my arms and down my spine. I try pulling Corey back the way we came, but nothing stops Corey, not even Lester's dog.

I pick up a stone and squeeze it in my fist. But even I know a little stone won't scare Lester's dog.

Corey gazes into the shadows under Lester's porch. Then he takes my hand and walks me straight past Lester's house.

I feel my heart squeezing up in my throat and my legs ready to run, but Lester's dog is too busy digging dust under his porch to notice me and Corey. Before I know it, we're past him, standing at the top of Garrison Avenue.

We look back, but Lester's dog is still under his porch, chewing dirt. I grin at Corey. "We made it," I say, swinging his hand. And Corey grins back.

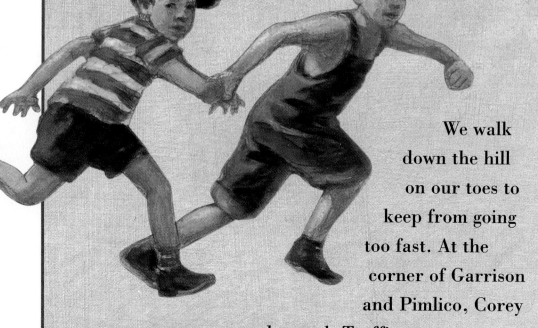

We walk down the hill on our toes to keep from going too fast. At the corner of Garrison and Pimlico, Corey gears up to cross the road. Traffic roars past, whipping up licks of my shirt that are not stuck down with sweat. I squeeze Corey's hand hard and he frowns, his head swiveling back and forth, back and forth, waiting for a good time to cross. And then there's a break in the traffic, and Corey pulls me off the curb. We fly over Pimlico Road like Lester's dog is chasing us.

Safely on the other side, Corey pulls me toward an old building. He stops at a wooden bulkhead.

"You brought me past Lester's dog for this?" I ask, squinting up into Corey's face. But then I hear something crying, and it's coming from beneath the bulkhead door.

Corey stoops down close to the pavement. The handle to the door is broken off, so he curls his fingers around the splintery edge and lifts it over his head. I shift back and forth from one foot to the other, trying to look past Corey into the shadows of the cellar way.

Then, on the steps, I see a tiny fist of fur, knotted up. I hear it mewing, mewing like a stuck record. Corey reaches in and scoops up a single kitten. He cups it to his ear like he was listening to the sea. One skinny paw catches in the wire of Corey's hearing aid but Corey doesn't mind. He just holds that kitten to his ear, listening.

I touch Corey's shoulder, and he looks at me real serious, then eases the kitten into my hands. I feel ribs and bones jutting up under scraggly fur. The kitten wriggles and turns in my fingers. It sucks at my sweaty shirt.

Corey lowers the wooden door and motions me
to follow him back home.

"We can't take this kitten," I say. "If we take it,
we've got to care for it."

But Corey doesn't hear, and even if he does I'm
not saying anything he doesn't already know. I try
to open the bulkhead myself to put the kitten back,
but Corey stamps his foot down on the wooden door.
He takes me by my elbow, leads me to the curb, and
with his fingers clamped on to me and me
clamped on to that kitten, we tear
back across Pimlico Road.

The kitten mews and mews in my hands. I tuck
it under my shirt so it will stop shivering. Its
rough tongue scrubs the same spot on my
stomach till it drives me crazy. I slip the
kitten back out and hold it
up close to my face.

"What are we going to do with you?" I ask. "I sure can't keep you. Mama says cats make her itch." The kitten's head tips to one side like it's listening to me, and I rub its fur against my cheek.

Before I know it, we're at the top of Garrison Avenue. And there, two lawns down, is Lester's dog, staring up at us and waiting.

Corey tries taking my hand, but my hands are full of kitten. So he starts down the hill first, looking straight ahead, and I follow.

Corey gets by all right and keeps going down the hill, but Lester's dog growls at me. He growls low and nasty. My legs feel like they're dragging bricks. The kitten starts mewing and shivering worse than ever.

For a second, everything is frozen like that—
Corey almost home, and me staring at Lester's dog,
and Lester's dog staring back. And then Lester's dog
comes unstuck, and he springs at me like I was some
old Chevy.

I run, holding tight to the kitten, and Lester's dog
snaps and snarls at my heels.

I am halfway down the hill, almost to Mr.
Frank's, when I feel Lester's dog slap my back with
his paws. My head whips around, and I struggle to
stay on my feet.

Lester's dog leaps up, barking and snapping, his eyes locked on the kitten. I lift the kitten higher, but Lester's dog grabs at my shirt, ripping it with his teeth.

All the times I've been scared is all bundled into right now. But suddenly what I'm feeling is not scared. What I'm feeling is mad!

A rumbling starts deep in my throat. I glare into that dog's face, and a sound rises up from a place inside of me I didn't know was there. My whole body fills with the sound and the ground seems to shake under me as I roar at Lester's dog.

And then Lester's dog is backing off. He's leaving, whining and slinking all the way up the block, crawling on his belly to hide under Lester's porch.

All of me is trembling, and my legs feel like loose Jell-O. I sit down on the curb waiting for the shaking to pass, holding tight to the kitten.

When I look up, Corey is beside me, gazing over his shoulder toward Mr. Frank's house. But Mr. Frank isn't in his chair anymore. He's standing on the porch and he's waving. I look at Corey and I know just what to do with that kitten after all.

Walking up the swept path, I reach out to Mr. Frank.

"Here, Mr. Frank," I say, pressing the kitten into his open hands.

Mr. Frank stands by the porch rail. He doesn't call after me. He doesn't ask any questions. He just stands there talking baby talk to that scrawny kitten.

203

Corey lays his arm across my shoulder and I reach up and lay my arm across his. We walk down the street and settle ourselves on my stoop.

I sit with Corey like that, slapping mosquitoes and watching while cars climb up the hill past Lester's house and drop home free down the other side, till Mama calls me in.

From the Author
Karen Hesse

Lester's Dog is a story about me. I was terrified of dogs when I was a child. But I overcame my fear, just as the boy in the story does. Now I have my own dog, a big black Labrador.

Corey, the friend in the story, is based on a friend of mine. We didn't speak to each other at all because, like Corey, my friend could not hear. Even though we didn't talk, we were still good pals. He read *Lester's Dog* and told me that he loved it.

Nancy Carpenter's illustrations are the perfect match for my story. Her drawings are so alive, and I love the colors.

I've probably been writing stories since the third or fourth grade. My teachers encouraged me. At that time I was wild about Dr. Seuss books. I would go to my neighborhood library and ask when the next book would be coming out.

I like to write many kinds of stories, but in one way or another, most of them are about my own childhood!

Karen Hesse

206

From the Illustrator
Nancy Carpenter

Lester's Dog was one of the first stories I ever illustrated. Because I loved Karen Hesse's story, the pictures were fun to draw. I felt the story was old-fashioned, so I decided to put the characters in a 1930s setting. I used colors that seemed golden and dusty, the way we might picture a small, old-fashioned town.

I did a lot of research for *Lester's Dog*. I decided that I wanted the dog to be sharp and pointy, so I took photographs of a lot of different dogs. I put those dogs together to come up with the scary, dirty dog that belonged to Lester.

Karen Hesse told me she was delighted with my illustrations. She had planned the main character as a girl, but as soon as I read the story I drew him as a boy. We didn't meet until all of my illustrations were complete.

I would tell anyone who wants to be an illustrator to practice drawing all the time. It isn't important to draw things so that they look real. It's important to have your own style. If you practice and practice, you will find out what that style is.

207

RESPONSE

SIGN YOUR NAME

Corey communicates with his friend without speaking. Today, many people who cannot speak or hear use American Sign Language. Part of this language is an alphabet of hand symbols. You can find this alphabet in most encyclopedias. Use the sign language alphabet to spell your name for your classmates.

BEWARE OF DOG!

Lester's dog probably scared a lot of neighborhood kids. What should you do if you meet a dangerous dog? Write two lists. One list should tell people what to do if they meet a dog they don't know. The other list should tell dog owners how to keep their dogs from hurting people. Share your lists with your class.

CORNER

A CHEERFUL PHONE CALL

Pets can be good company for people who live alone. Show how happy Mr. Frank is about his new pet. Write what he and a good friend say on the telephone. Have them talk about Mr. Frank's feelings and about how he should care for the kitten. Then act out their telephone talk with a partner.

WHAT DO YOU THINK?

- Why does Corey make his friend walk past Lester's dog?

- How did you feel when the boy who was holding the kitten roared at Lester's dog? Why?

- Think about Mr. Frank's problem. How do you think having a kitten might help him?

209

from *Current Health 1* magazine

Tony felt discouraged. Even though he had studied hard for his last math test, he still got a bad grade. Now another big test was coming up, and he was worried that he wasn't going to do well again. Maybe, he thought, he shouldn't even bother to study.

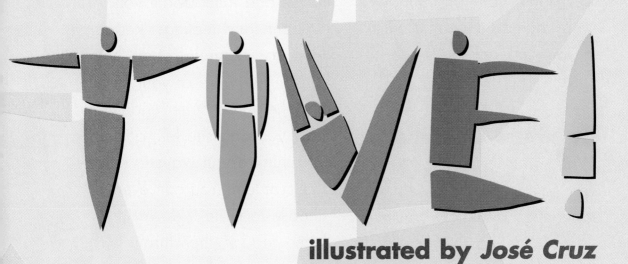

illustrated by José Cruz

It's easy to lose your confidence at times and think that you won't do well. How you think about something, however, can affect how well you do. Scientists have studied the way our bodies and minds work together. They've found that our thoughts can affect our bodies just as our bodies can affect our thoughts.

Have you ever played a game and noticed how you try harder or run faster when your friends start to cheer for you? If you are having a good day or are in a good mood, doesn't it seem easier to do your work, try new things, or not get so upset about a problem? All these are times when you're aware of your body and mind working together.

MAKE IT HAPPEN

But you don't have to wait until you are in a good mood or have your friends cheer for you to do better. You can control how you think. When bad thoughts start to make you feel worried or discouraged, you can change them by doing things that will help you think and act more positively.

Here are some ideas:

• *Write it down.* Maybe you have a journal or diary or have tried writing down how you feel in a letter. Writing can help in a lot of ways. One is that you are

able to get all those bad ideas out of your head, instead of thinking and thinking and getting upset. It's like talking to a friend about what is bothering you. You usually feel better after you do. Writing also gives you a chance to read what you wrote and think about your thoughts and feelings. Reading later, for example, about how angry you were at your sister may help you better understand how you and she felt, or help you think about ways to solve the problem. You can even choose to write it down in a letter, read it, then throw it away—instead of mailing it!

• *Talk to yourself.* Thinking is a way of talking to ourselves, and how we talk to ourselves affects how we feel. When we're in a bad mood, we say things to ourselves like "I can't do it," "It isn't fair," "I don't care." Talking to ourselves like this just makes our bad feelings worse. Listen and pay attention to what you

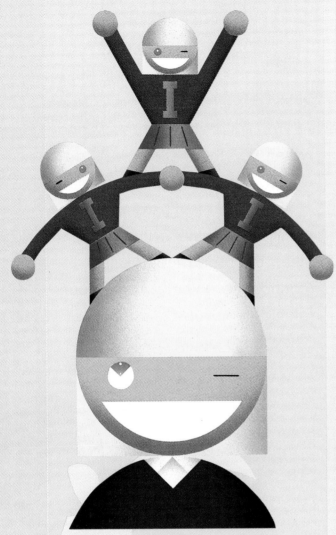

• *Imagine.* Have you ever looked forward to a trip and imagined all the wonderful things you hope will happen? It's hard not to get excited. You can do the same thing to help yourself when you're having a hard time. Imagine yourself doing well. Tony, for example, can imagine himself taking that test and breezing through the questions, or he can imagine his teacher handing him back his test with a great grade on it. Before a game, professional athletes often imagine themselves playing a perfect game. Imagining in this way gives you energy to keep trying, helps you learn better, and can make you feel like you will succeed.

say to yourself. If you catch yourself thinking negative things, try changing them to positive ones. Use other words like "I can," "I know I can do it," "I can solve the problem," "It's OK to make a mistake," "I can get help." It's like having a cheering team inside yourself to help you do better.

• *Find the solution.* It's easy sometimes to worry more about the problem than to think about a solution, but that usually only keeps you upset. If, for example, you think a lot about how badly your team played in the last game, or how awful you were in the school play, you'll feel crummy and won't know how to do better next time. It's OK to make mistakes; they tell us what we need to learn. Use them to figure out what you need to improve, and come up with a plan to do it. If you need help or some good ideas, talk to your parents, teachers, or friends.

GETTING STARTED

Once you start to think positively, it's hard to stop it. You'll start to feel better, and when you feel better, you'll do better. People around you will notice, and they'll say positive things to you that will help keep that good mood and confidence. What's more, your attitude can rub off on them. They'll like being around you

and may learn from you about how to handle hard times.

Like most new things, learning to think positively takes some practice. It may seem hard or awkward when you first start to write down your feelings or try to imagine positive situations. You may feel it won't help to talk to yourself differently or think up solutions, especially when you are having a hard time.

Don't try to change too quickly. Start slowly; pick one or two of the ideas to try. Ask your teacher or parent to help you recognize when bad thinking is getting you down or to encourage you to think positive. Talk to friends who have a good attitude, and ask them how they keep it up. Most of all, don't get discouraged. Think positive—you can learn to do it! ☺

My Name Is María Isabel

by Alma Flor Ada
illustrated by Leslie Wu

Award-Winning Author

María Isabel Salazar López is proud of her name, because she is named for her relatives. She has two problems, though. Her teacher calls her Mary López, because there are too many other Marías in the class. Also, María does not have a part in the class's Winter Pageant, because the teacher called on Mary López when she assigned parts and María didn't respond. Every day the pageant draws closer and closer, and she knows her parents are eager to see her in the show.

Everything at school now revolved around plans for the Winter Pageant. The class was making wreaths and lanterns. The teacher explained to the class that Christmas is celebrated differently in different countries, and that many people don't celebrate Christmas at all. They talked about Santa Claus, and how he is called Saint Nicholas in some countries and Father Christmas in others. The class

217

also talked about the Jewish feast of Hanukkah that celebrates the rededication of the Temple of Jerusalem, and about the special meaning of the nine candles of the Hanukkah menorah.

The teacher had asked everyone to bring in pictures or other things having to do with the holidays. A lot of kids brought in photographs of their families by their Christmas trees. Mayra brought in pictures of New Year's Day in Santo Domingo. Michelle brought in a picture of herself sitting on Santa's lap when she was little. Gabriel brought in photos of the Three Kings' Day parade in Miami, Florida. He had been there last year, when he went to visit his Cuban grandmother. Marcos brought in a piñata shaped like a green parrot that his uncle had brought back from Mexico. Emmanuel showed everyone a photo album of his family's trip to Israel, and Esther brought in cards her grandfather had sent her from Jerusalem.

One day, Suni Paz came to the school. She sang Christmas songs from different countries and taught the class to sing a Hanukkah song, "The Candles of Hanukkah."

María Isabel went home humming softly "Hanukkah . . . Hanukkah . . . Let us celebrate." The bus trip seemed a lot shorter as the song ran through her head. It almost felt as if she had traveled to all those different countries and had celebrated all those different holidays.

María Isabel was still singing while she made dinner and set the table:

"With our menorah,
Fine potato latkes,
Our clay trumpets,
Let us celebrate."

Her voice filled the empty kitchen. María Isabel was so pleased she promised herself that she'd make a snowman the next time it snowed. And she'd get it finished before the garbage men picked up the trash and dirtied up the snow.

But after Suni Paz's visit to the school, the days seemed to drag by more and more slowly. María Isabel didn't have anything to do during rehearsals, since she didn't have a part in *Amahl*.

The teacher decided that after the play the actors would sing some holiday songs, including María Isabel's favorite about the Hanukkah candles. Since she didn't have a part, María Isabel wouldn't be asked to sing either.

It didn't seem to matter much to Tony and Jonathan, the other two kids who weren't in the play. They spent rehearsal time reading comics or whispering to each other. Neither boy spoke to María Isabel, and she was too shy to say anything to them.

The only fun she had was reading her library book. Somehow her problems seemed so small compared to Wilbur the pig's. He was in danger of becoming the holiday dinner. María Isabel felt the only difference was that the characters in books always seemed to find answers to their problems, while she couldn't figure out what to do about her own.

As she cut out bells and stars for decorations, María Isabel daydreamed about being a famous singer. Someday she would sing in front of a large audience, and her teacher would feel guilty that she had not let María Isabel sing in the Winter Pageant.

But later María Isabel thought, My teacher isn't so bad. It's all a big misunderstanding. . . . If only there was some way I could let her know. Even if I'm not a great singer someday, it doesn't matter. All I really want is to be myself and not make the teacher angry all the time. I just want to be in the play and to be called María Isabel Salazar López.

"**I**'ve asked my boss if I can leave work early the day of the school pageant," María Isabel's mother said one evening as she served the soup. "Papá is also going to leave work early. That way we'll be able to bring the rice and beans."

"And best of all, we can hear María Isabel sing," her father added.

María Isabel looked down at her soup. She had not told her parents anything. She knew they were going to be very disappointed when they saw the other kids in her class taking part in the play. She could just hear her mother asking, "Why didn't you sing? Doesn't the teacher know what a lovely voice you have?" María Isabel ate her soup in silence. What could she say?

"Don't you have anything to say, Chabelita?" asked her father. "Aren't you glad we're coming?"

"Sure, Papá, sure I am," said María Isabel, and she got up to take her empty bowl to the sink.

After helping her mother with the dishes, María Isabel went straight to her room. She put on her pajamas and got into bed. But she couldn't sleep, so she turned the light on and continued reading *Charlotte's Web*. María Isabel felt that she was caught in a sticky, troublesome spider's web of her own, and the more she tried to break loose, the more trapped she became.

When the librarian had told her that she would like the book, María Isabel had felt that they were sharing a secret. Now as she turned the pages, she thought that maybe the secret was that *everyone* has problems. She felt close to poor little Wilbur, being fattened up for Christmas dinner without even knowing it. He was a little like her parents, who were so eager to go to the pageant, not knowing what was waiting for them.

"It just isn't fair that this can't be a happy time for all of us!" María Isabel said out loud. She sighed. Then she turned off the light, snuggled under her blanket, and fell asleep trying to figure out a way to save Wilbur from becoming Christmas dinner.

Two days were left until the pageant. The morning was cloudy and gray. On the way to school, María Isabel wondered if it was going to snow. Maybe she would be able to make that snowman. But shortly after she got to school, it started to drizzle.

Since they couldn't go outside, the students spent their time rehearsing. No one made a mistake. Melchior didn't forget what he had to say to Amahl's mother.

Amahl dropped his crutch only once. Best of all, though, the shepherds remembered when they were supposed to enter, without bumping into the Three Kings.

Even Tony and Jonathan seemed interested in the play. They volunteered to help carry the manger and the shepherds' baskets on- and offstage.

Satisfied with the final rehearsal, the teacher decided there was time for one last class exercise before vacation. "It's been a couple of days since we've done some writing," she said when the students returned to class. "The new year is a time for wishes. Sometimes wishes come true; sometimes they don't. But it's important to have wishes and, most of all, to know what you really want. I'd like you all to take out some paper and write an essay titled 'My Greatest Wish.' "

María Isabel sighed and put away *Charlotte's Web.* Charlotte had just died, and María Isabel wondered what was going to happen to the sac of eggs that Wilbur had saved, and when Charlotte's babies would be born. But María Isabel would have to wait to find out. She bit down on her pencil and wrote: "My greatest wish . . ."

This shouldn't be so hard, María Isabel thought. If I finish writing early, I can probably finish my book. She started to write: "My greatest wish is to make a snowman. . . ."

María Isabel read over what she had just written, and realized that it wasn't what she really wanted. She put the paper aside, took out a new sheet, and wrote down the title again. "My greatest wish is to have a part in *Amahl. . . .*"

María Isabel stopped writing again. She thought, Would Charlotte have said that her greatest wish was to save Wilbur? Or would she have wished for something impossible, like living until the next spring and getting to know her children? The teacher just said that wishes don't always come true. If I'm going to wish for something, it should be something really worth wishing for.

María Isabel took out a third sheet of paper and wrote down the title again. This time, she didn't stop writing until she got to the bottom of the page.

My Greatest Wish

When I started to write I thought my greatest wish was to make a snowman. Then I thought my greatest wish was to have a part in the Winter Pageant. But I think my greatest wish is to be called María Isabel Salazar López. When that was my name, I felt proud of being named María like my papá's mother, and Isabel, like my grandmother Chabela. She is saving money so that I can study and not have to spend my whole life in a kitchen like her. I was Salazar like my papá and my grandpa Antonio, and López, like my grandfather Manuel. I never knew him but he could really tell stories. I know because my mother told me.

If I was called María Isabel Salazar López, I could listen better in class because it's easier to hear than Mary López. Then I could have said that I wanted a part in the play. And when the rest of the kids sing, my mother and father wouldn't have to ask me why I didn't sing, even though I like the song about the Hanukkah candles so much.

The rest of the class had already handed in their essays and were cleaning out their desks to go home when María Isabel got up. She quietly went to the front of the room and put her essay on the teacher's desk. María Isabel didn't look up at the teacher, so she didn't see the woman smiling at her. She hurried back to her desk to get her things and leave.

Holiday spirit was everywhere at school the next day. The paper wreaths and lanterns the class had made were hung up all over the room. The teacher had put the "greatest wish" essays up on the bulletin board, next to the cutouts of Santa Claus, the Three Kings, and a menorah.

All the students were restless. Marta Pérez smiled when María Isabel sat down next to her. "Look at the pretty Christmas card I got from my cousin in Santo Domingo," she said excitedly. María Isabel looked at the tropical Christmas scene, all trimmed in flowers. But she couldn't answer Marta because the teacher had started to speak.

"We're going to do one last rehearsal because there's a small change in the program."

The rest of the kids listened attentively, but María Isabel just kept looking down at her desk. After all, she had nothing to do with the pageant.

Then she heard the teacher say, "María Isabel, María Isabel Salazar López . . ." María Isabel looked up in amazement.

"Wouldn't you like to lead the song about the Hanukkah candles?" the teacher said with a wide grin. "Why don't you start by yourself, and then everyone else can join in. Go ahead and start when you're ready."

María Isabel walked nervously up to the front of the room and stood next to the teacher, who was strumming her guitar. Then she took a deep breath and began to sing her favorite holiday song.

While her mother was getting the rice and beans ready that night, Mr. Salazar called María Isabel over to him. "Since you can't wear makeup yet, Chabelita, I've brought you something else that I think you'll like." In the palm of his hand were two barrettes for her hair. They were shaped like butterflies and gleamed with tiny stones.

"Oh, Papi. They're so pretty! Thank you!" María Isabel exclaimed. She hugged her father and ran to her room to put them on.

At school the next day, María Isabel stood in the center of the stage. She was wearing her special yellow dress, a pair of new shoes, and the shining butterflies. She spoke clearly to the audience. "My name is María Isabel Salazar López. I'm going to sing a song about the Jewish feast of Hanukkah, that celebrates the rededication of the Temple in Jerusalem." The music started, and María Isabel began to sing:

The Candles of Hanukkah

One little candle,
Two little candles,
Three little candles,
Let us celebrate.
Four little candles,
Five little candles,
Six little candles,
Let us celebrate.
Hanukkah, Hanukkah,
Let us celebrate.
Seven little candles,
Eight little candles,
Nine little candles,
Let us celebrate.
Hanukkah, Hanukkah,
Let us celebrate.
With our menorah,
Fine potato latkes,
Our clay trumpets,
Let us celebrate.
With our family,
With our friends,
With our presents,
Let us celebrate.

And the butterflies in María Isabel's hair sparkled under the stage lights so much that it seemed that they might just take off and fly.

A Note from the Author
Alma Flor Ada

grandmother chose the name Almaflor for me. My family wanted it to be written as one word. Since in Spanish *Alma* means "soul," and *flor* means "flower," it is quite an unusual name.

Unfortunately, on my birth certificate, the clerk spelled the name as two words instead of one. When I started third grade, the teacher told me to spell my name as it was on my birth certificate. Even today I am sorry I listened to that teacher. I liked my special name. It was different from other children's, but it had been chosen with love for me, and it was mine.

There is a second reason I wrote this book. When I visit schools, I often hear people saying children's names wrong.

W̳hat are the reasons behind writing a book? Authors are not always sure. I think I wrote *My Name Is María Isabel* for two different reasons. One has to do with my own name. My mother's name is Alma. When I was born, my

Children are sometimes embarrassed to speak up, but they should not be. We should respect each other's names, as we should respect each other.

I wrote *My Name Is María Isabel* in Spanish first. Here is a page from the *third* draft of the book. In case you don't read Spanish, I should tell you that this is the part where María Isabel is about to sing in the winter pageant.

Notice that I made several changes to this draft, even though it wasn't a first draft. Some people think that authors just sit down and write until they're finished. That's certainly not true! The best authors I know keep making changes and corrections until their writing is the best it can be.

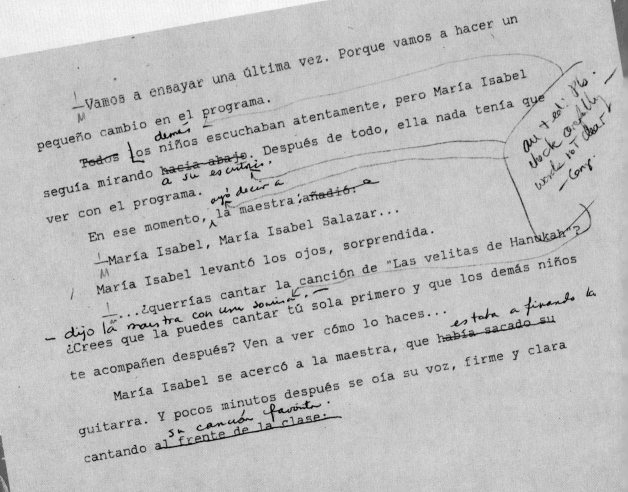

How a Girl Got Her Chinese Name

by Nellie Wong

On the first day of school the teacher asked me:
What do your parents call you at home?

I answered: Nellie.

Nellie? Nellie?
The teacher stressed the *l*'s, whinnying like a horse.
No such name in Chinese for a name like Nellie.
We shall call you *Nah Lei*[1]
which means *Where* or *Which Place*.

The teacher brushed my new name,
black on beige paper.
I practiced writing *Nah Lei*
holding the brush straight, dipping
the ink over and over.

After school I ran home.
Papa, Mama, the teacher says my name is *Nah Lei*.
I did not look my parents in the eye.

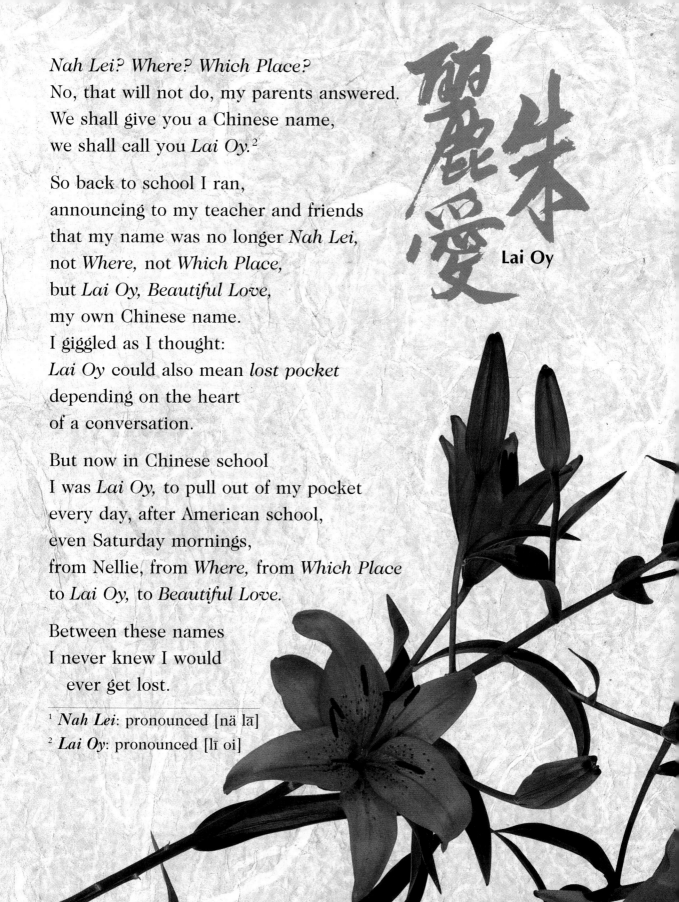

Nah Lei? Where? Which Place?
No, that will not do, my parents answered.
We shall give you a Chinese name,
we shall call you *Lai Oy.*[2]

So back to school I ran,
announcing to my teacher and friends
that my name was no longer *Nah Lei,*
not *Where,* not *Which Place,*
but *Lai Oy, Beautiful Love,*
my own Chinese name.
I giggled as I thought:
Lai Oy could also mean *lost pocket*
depending on the heart
of a conversation.

But now in Chinese school
I was *Lai Oy,* to pull out of my pocket
every day, after American school,
even Saturday mornings,
from Nellie, from *Where,* from *Which Place*
to *Lai Oy,* to *Beautiful Love.*

Between these names
I never knew I would
    ever get lost.

Lai Oy

---

[1] *Nah Lei*: pronounced [nä lā]
[2] *Lai Oy*: pronounced [lī oi]

Who Is Special?

Everyone is special. Make a poster that tells about you. Include a photo of yourself. Then spell out your name and decorate it. You can use colored markers, yarn, glitter, or anything else. Then, from magazines, cut out pictures and words that show what you are like. Share your poster with your classmates.

Response Corner

Where Did You Get Your Name?

María Isabel Salazar López and the girl in "How a Girl Got Her Chinese Name" thought their names were special. Find out whether your family has a special naming custom. Ask your parents or grandparents. Write a list of important family names, and tell why they are important.

Holiday Treasures

The Winter Pageant showed how different holidays are celebrated around the world. Bring in a picture or another item that helps to show how you and your family celebrate a holiday. Tell a friend why the picture or other item is special.

What Do You Think?

- How does María Isabel solve her problems?

- Do you think María Isabel is brave? Explain your answer.

- It can be hard to start in a new school. What are some things you could do to help a new student in your school?

235

THEME WRAP-UP

The characters in this theme discover different kinds of courage. How do other people help them be brave? Do any of the characters help other people? How?

Which character in this theme is the bravest? Support your answer with reasons and examples.

ACTIVITY CORNER

Has anyone ever helped you to be brave? Maybe someone gave you advice, or maybe you just followed someone's example. Write a thank-you note to the person who helped you, and explain what you have learned about bravery.

Glossary

WHAT IS A GLOSSARY?

A glossary is like a small dictionary at the back of a book. It lists some of the words used in the book, along with their pronunciations, their meanings, and other useful information. If you come across a word you don't know as you are reading, you can look up the word in this glossary.

Using the

Like a dictionary, this glossary lists words in alphabetical order. To find a word, look it up by its first letter or letters.

To save time, use the **guide words** at the top of each page. These show you the first and last words on the page. Look at the guide words to see if your word falls between them alphabetically.

Here is an example of a glossary entry:

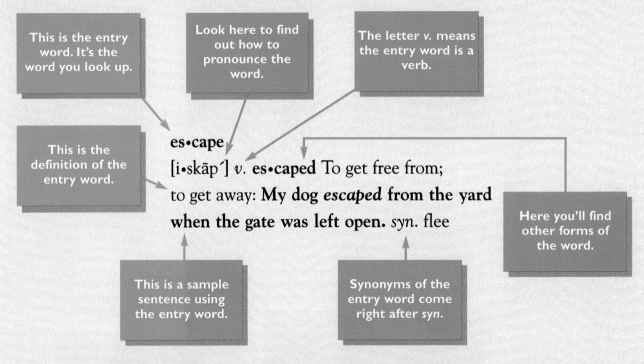

This is the entry word. It's the word you look up.

Look here to find out how to pronounce the word.

The letter *v.* means the entry word is a verb.

This is the definition of the entry word.

es•cape
[i•skāp´] *v.* **es•caped** To get free from; to get away: **My dog** *escaped* **from the yard when the gate was left open.** *syn.* flee

Here you'll find other forms of the word.

This is a sample sentence using the entry word.

Synonyms of the entry word come right after *syn.*

ETYMOLOGY

Etymology is the study or history of how words are developed. Words often have interesting backgrounds that can help you remember what they mean. Look in the margins of the glossary to find the etymologies of certain words.

Here is an example of an etymology:

crane *Crane* is also the name of a long-necked bird. The big machine used for lifting heavy things got its name because it looks like the bird.

Glossary

PRONUNCIATION

The pronunciation in brackets is a respelling that shows how the word is pronounced.

The **pronunciation key** explains what the symbols in a respelling mean. A shortened pronunciation key appears on every other page of the glossary.

PRONUNCIATION KEY*

a	add, map	m	move, seem	u	up, done		
ā	ace, rate	n	nice, tin	û(r)	burn, term		
â(r)	care, air	ng	ring, song	yo͞o	fuse, few		
ä	palm, father	o	odd, hot	v	vain, eve		
b	bat, rub	ō	open, so	w	win, away		
ch	check, catch	ô	order, jaw	y	yet, yearn		
d	dog, rod	oi	oil, boy	z	zest, muse		
e	end, pet	ou	pout, now	zh	vision, pleasure		
ē	equal, tree	o͝o	took, full	ə	the schwa, an		
f	fit, half	o͞o	pool, food		unstressed vowel		
g	go, log	p	pit, stop		representing the		
h	hope, hate	r	run, poor		sound spelled		
i	it, give	s	see, pass		*a* in *above*		
ī	ice, write	sh	sure, rush		*e* in *sicken*		
j	joy, ledge	t	talk, sit		*i* in *possible*		
k	cool, take	th	thin, both		*o* in *melon*		
l	look, rule	t̶h̶	this, bathe		*u* in *circus*		

Other symbols:
• separates words into syllables
ˊ indicates heavier stress on a syllable
ˏ indicates light stress on a syllable

Abbreviations: *adj.* adjective, *adv.* adverb, *conj.* conjunction, *interj.* interjection, *n.* noun, *prep.* preposition, *pron.* pronoun, *syn.* synonym, *v.* verb.

active The words *active*, *act*, *action*, and *actor* all come from a Latin word meaning "to do or perform." However, *player* was used in the theater until the sixteenth century, when it changed to *actor*.

advise *Advise* comes from a Latin word meaning "in my view." The French gave it the meaning "in my opinion." In English, it means "to give information."

a•chiev•er

[ə•chēv´er] *n.* Someone who does what he or she tries to do; someone who reaches a goal: **Teresa is a high achiever because she does her best and gets good grades.**

ac•tive

[ak´tiv] *adj.* Working; busy; full of life and doing things: **Owls sleep during the day and are active at night.**

ad•vise

[ad•vīz´] *v.* To tell someone what to do or how to do it: **The coach is going to advise his players about how to hit a baseball.**
syns. recommend; inform

an•kle

[ang´kəl] *n.* **an•kles** The bony area between a person's leg and foot: **It had rained all afternoon, and the puddles were up to Misha's ankles.**

a•ware

[ə•wâr´] *adj.* In a state of knowing; understanding fully: **Tracy was not aware that the car was coming toward her, until her friend shouted to her.**
syn. alert

cap•ture

[kap´chər] *v.* To catch: **Josh knew not to capture the beautiful butterfly because there are too few of them left already.** *syns.* take; trap

ca•reer

[kə•rir´] *n.* A person's life work; a job one trains for or studies for and then does for a long time: **Ahmad had an interesting** *career* **as an author of children's books.**

cel•e•brate

[sel´ə•brāt´] *v.* **cel•e•brat•ed** To take part in a holiday activity or a party: **We** *celebrated* **the Fourth of July with music and ice cream.**
syns. observe; rejoice

con•cen•trate

[kon´sən•trāt´] *v.* To pay attention to only one thing; to think about something very hard: **When I study my science lesson, I need to** *concentrate.*
syn. focus

coun•try•side

[kun´trē•sīd´] *n.* Land outside the city: **The** *countryside* **is pretty because lots of trees and grass cover the land.**

cous•in

[kuz´(ə)n] *n.* **cous•ins** Something or someone that is like or in the same family as another: **Even though large pandas look like bears, pandas are actually** *cousins* **of the raccoon.**

crane

[krān] *n.* A big tractor-like machine with a long arm used to lift and move things: **They used a** *crane* **to lift the heavy pole and put it in a truck that would take it away.**

cun•ning

[kun´ing] *adj.* Clever and tricky; smart in a sneaky way: **My cat is very** *cunning* **and will drink your milk when you are not looking.**

cunning

countryside

crane *Crane* is also the name of a long-necked bird. The big machine used for lifting heavy things got its name because it looks like the bird.

a	add	o͝o	took
ā	ace	o͞o	pool
â	care	u	up
ä	palm	û	burn
e	end	yo͞o	fuse
ē	equal	oi	oil
i	it	ou	pout
ī	ice	ng	ring
o	odd	th	thin
ō	open	t͟h	this
ô	order	zh	vision

ə = {
a in *above*
e in *sicken*
i in *possible*
o in *melon*
u in *circus*

337

damage The English word is the same as the original French word *damage*. But the French changed it to *dommage*.

daydream

D

dam•age
[dam´ij] *n.* The hurt caused by an action; a loss of or harm to something: **The fire caused a lot of *damage* to the barn.** *syn.* injury

day•dream
[dā´drēm´] *v.* **day•dreamed** To imagine nice thoughts or wishes; to think about pleasant ideas in a wishful way: **Latisha *daydreamed* about the great things she will do when she grows up.**

de•pend
[di•pend´] *v.* To trust; to need someone or something: **I *depend* on you to help your little sister with her homework.** *syn.* rely

des•ert
[dez´ərt] *n.* A very dry place that may be covered with sand and has few plants: **The *desert* is very hot in the daytime, but it cools down at night.**

dif•fer•ent•ly
[dif´ə•rənt•lē] *adv.* Not in the same way: **Juan combs his hair *differently* than his twin does, and it helps people tell them apart.** *syn.* distinctly

dis•ap•pear
[dis´ə•pir´] *v.* **dis•ap•peared** To go out of sight: **Betty watched as the plane *disappeared* into the sky.** *syn.* vanish

dis•ap•point•ed
[dis´ə•point´id] *adj.* Not getting what you wanted or hoped for; let down; feeling unhappy: **Susan was *disappointed* that the rain kept her from going outside.** *syn.* dissatisfied

drab

[drab] *adj.* Boring looking; uninteresting or dull in color: **Other people said the weather was *drab*, but Dennis loved the gray, rainy days.**

drift

[drift] *v.* **drift•ed** To move back and forth slowly through the air: **The leaves *drifted* down from the trees.**

dusk

[dusk] *n.* The time just before night falls; after sunset and before dark: **All the streetlights go on at *dusk*, before it gets too dark.**

e•lec•tric•i•ty

[i•lek´tris´ə•tē] *n.* Something that gives power to make things work; the flow of charges through a substance, such as a wire, used to run things: ***Electricity* is used to keep our stove and refrigerator going.**

es•cape

[i•skāp´] *v.* **es•caped** To get free from; to get away: **My dog *escaped* from the yard when the gate was left open.** *syn.* flee

fault

[fôlt] *n.* The cause of a problem: **The bus was late, so it was not our *fault* we missed the school bell.** *syn.* blame

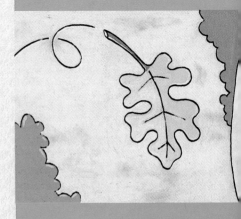

escape *Escape* comes from a Latin word meaning "to take off one's coat." The English decided it means "to get one's freedom."

a	add	ŏŏ	took
ā	ace	ōō	pool
â	care	u	up
ä	palm	û	burn
e	end	yōō	fuse
ē	equal	oi	oil
i	it	ou	pout
ī	ice	ng	ring
o	odd	th	thin
ō	open	t͟h	this
ô	order	zh	vision

ə = { *a* in *above*
e in *sicken*
i in *possible*
o in *melon*
u in *circus*

339

fortune

fortune The Roman god of luck was called *Fortuna*. If she was on your side, you were considered *fortunate*.

harbor

jewel

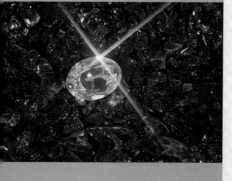

for·tune

[fôr´chən] *n.* **for·tunes**
Luck or chance; success; wealth: **After finishing high school, they left the farm to find their** *fortunes* **in the big city.**

fright·en

[frīt´ən] *v.* **fright·ened**
To make afraid; to be made afraid: **The baby was** *frightened* **by the loud noises.** *syn.* scare

fro·zen

[frō´zən] *adj.* Not moving; being still: **When he saw the bear, he stood** *frozen* **in his tracks.**

H

har·bor

[här´bər] *n.* A part of the ocean, near land, where ships stay and are safe: **As the storm rolled in, more ships sailed into the** *harbor* **to be safe.** *syn.* port

I

im·i·tate

[im´ə·tāt´] *v.* To copy something to make it look the same; to use as an example: **Brad liked the way his brother danced and tried to** *imitate* **him at the party.** *syn.* mimic

im·pos·si·ble

[im·pos´ə·bəl] *adj.* Unable to be done; not able to happen: **It's** *impossible* **to be in two places at one time.** *syn.* unworkable

J

jew·el

[jōō´əl] *n.* A stone that is usually worth money; something that is worth a lot: **The ring with the bright red** *jewel* **in it cost a lot of money.**

L

light•ning

[līt´ning] *n.* A sudden bright flash in the sky caused by an electrical charge from storm clouds: **The weather report said there would be a lot of** *lightning* **during the storm.**

P

pack•age

[pak´ij] *n.* Something that is wrapped up or boxed: **Mario was able to fit the card into the large** *package* **of fruit that was being sent to his grandparents.**

pas•ture

[pas´chər] *n.* Ground covered with grass for animals to eat: **From the road, Minh could see cows eating in a** *pasture.*

pe•ti•tion

[pə•tish´ən] *n.* A paper people can sign that asks for something from someone in charge: **The students have a** *petition* **asking the school for more computers.**

pho•to•graph

[fō´tə•graf´] *n.* **pho•to•graphs** A picture made with a camera: **We took lots of** *photographs* **of the Grand Canyon on our vacation to Arizona.**

lightning

photograph
Photograph comes from *photo,* meaning "light," and *graph,* meaning "write." Photography is something like "writing with light."

a	add	o͝o	took
ā	ace	o͞o	pool
â	care	u	up
ä	palm	û	burn
e	end	yo͞o	fuse
ē	equal	oi	oil
i	it	ou	pout
ī	ice	ng	ring
o	odd	th	thin
ō	open	t̶h̶	this
ô	order	zh	vision

ə = {
  a in *above*
  e in *sicken*
  i in *possible*
  o in *melon*
  u in *circus*

pluck

property

realize *Realize* comes from the word *real*. In English *real* was first used to mean "property," and that is where we get the term *real estate*. Later, *real* took on the meaning of "something that actually exists."

pluck

[pluk] *v.* To pull off; to pull out: **I *pluck* the flowers from the garden and put them in a vase.** *syn.* pick

plump

[plump] *adj.* A little fat; having a rounded shape: **The little piglets were *plump*, just like their mother.** *syn.* chubby

pro·gram

[prō´gram´] *n.* A planned way to do something; steps to follow to do something; an organized activity: **Phyllis is going to join the after-school basketball *program*.** *syns.* procedure, organization

prop·er·ty

[prop´ər·tē] *n.* A piece of land; something owned by a person or a group: **The *property* our house is on is small, so we do not have a big yard.** *syn.* holdings

R

re·al·ize

[rē´əl·īz´] *v.* **re·al·ized** To understand; to come to know: **They *realized* the big dog was really very friendly, even though it barked loudly.**

re·call

[ri·kôl´] *v.* To remember; to think about again; to bring to mind again: **Debbie tried to *recall* where she had left her book.** *syn.* recollect

re·cord

[rek´ərd] *n.* **re·cords**
Information about a
person or business:
**School *records* tell
about the students,
their grades, and their
behavior.** *syn.* document

rel·a·tive

[rel´ə·tiv] *n.* **rel·a·tives**
A person in the same
family: **My aunts, my
uncles, and all of my
other *relatives* brought
me presents when they
came to my birthday
party.** *syn.* kin

re·spon·si·ble

[ri·spon´sə·bəl] *adj.*
Being the cause of
something; being the
person in charge of
something: **Tomika is
responsible for having
made the signs too small,
and she will fix them.**

sci·en·tist

[sī´ən·tist] *n.* **sci·en·tists**
A person who studies
nature and life: **Some
scientists study the
Earth, the stars, the
moon, and the sun.**

shad·ow

[shad´ō] *n.* **shad·ows**
A dark area, where light
is cut off: **The tree
blocks the sun, so we
keep cool by sitting in
the *shadows* underneath
the tree.** *syn.* shade

shiv·er

[shiv´ər] *v.* **shiv·ered** To
shake from fear or cold:
**In the spooky old
house, Curtis *shivered*
when he heard strange
noises outside his door.**

soar

[sôr] *v.* **soar·ing** To fly
high: **The kite was
soaring high in the air.**

scientist

shadow *Shadow*
comes from *shade*,
which is related to
the word *shed. Shed*
used to mean "a
roof held up by
poles." In hot
weather, one would
go under a *shed* to
get in the *shade.*

a	add	o͝o	took
ā	ace	o͞o	pool
â	care	u	up
ä	palm	û	burn
e	end	yo͞o	fuse
ē	equal	oi	oil
i	it	ou	pout
ī	ice	ng	ring
o	odd	th	thin
ō	open	t͟h	this
ô	order	zh	vision

ə = { a in *above*
e in *sicken*
i in *possible*
o in *melon*
u in *circus*

343

squeeze

sunset

spar·kle

[spar´kəl] *v.* **spar·kling**
To shine; to glitter:
**Everyone in the room
could see her crown**
sparkling **as she danced
with the prince.** *syns.*
glisten, twinkle

sprin·kle

[spring´kəl] *v.* **sprin·kling**
To drop or throw tiny
pieces around gently: **Ted
likes** *sprinkling* **cheese
on his chili.** *syn.* scatter

squeeze

[skwēz] *v.* To press; to
push together: **I like to**
squeeze **oranges in
order to make fresh
orange juice.** *syn.* crush

stub·born

[stub´ərn] *adj.* Not
willing to change one's
mind; not giving in:
Diane was so *stubborn*
**that she would not
even try the new game.**
syn. unbending

suc·cess

[sək·ses´] *n.* The state of
getting good results; a
person who is good at
something or is well
known: **When Darnell
won the spelling bee,
he knew he was a**
success.

sun·set

[sun´set´] n. The time
when the sun goes
down, just before it
turns dark: **At** *sunset,*
**we pick up our toys
and go inside.**

tear

[târ] *v.* **tears** To move
very fast: **Greg** *tears*
**down the street on his
bicycle in a hurry to
meet his friends.**
syns. race, rush

thun·der

[thun´dər] *n.* The loud booming sound that comes from the sky during a storm: **Our dog hid under the bed because the *thunder* scared him.**

tum·ble·weed

[tum´bəl·wēd´] *n.* **tum·ble·weeds** A round bush that grows in flat, dry areas without trees and that, when dead, is blown around by the wind: **The *tumbleweeds* had dried up and were light, so the wind blew them across the ranch and into the fence.**

van·ish

[van´ish] *v.* To go out of sight: **As soon as my dog heard the bathwater running, he would *vanish*.** *syn.* disappear

weave

[wēv] *v.* To make something by crossing long pieces of material, such as cloth or rope, over and under each other: **Rosa's grandmother showed her how to *weave* a rug out of strips of cloth.**

weave

thunder *Thunder* comes from a word meaning "noise." Thor was the Nordic god of thunder who drove his chariot across the sky with a great rumbling noise. A day was named after him. *Thursday* is "Thor's day."

tumbleweed

a	add	oͦo	took
ā	ace	ōͦo	pool
â	care	u	up
ä	palm	û	burn
e	end	yōͦo	fuse
ē	equal	oi	oil
i	it	ou	pout
ī	ice	ng	ring
o	odd	th	thin
ō	open	th	this
ô	order	zh	vision

ə = {
  a in *above*
  e in *sicken*
  i in *possible*
  o in *melon*
  u in *circus*
}

INDEX OF
Titles and Authors

Page numbers in color refer to biographical information.

Acknowledgements

For permission to reprint copyrighted material, grateful acknowledgment is made to the following sources:

Atheneum Books for Young Readers, an imprint of Simon & Schuster: Edited manuscript page from *Me Llamo María Isabel* by Alma Flor Ada. Text copyright © 1993 by Alma Flor Ada. From *My Name Is María Isabel* by Alma Flor Ada, translated from the Spanish by Ana M. Cerro. Text copyright © 1993 by Alma Flor Ada; "The Candles of Hanukkah" copyright © 1990 by Suni Paz (ASCAP).

August House, Inc.: "The Turnip: A Russian Tale" from *Twenty-Two Splendid Tales to Tell from Around the World*, Volume One by Pleasant DeSpain. Text and cover illustration © 1979, 1990, 1994 by Pleasant DeSpain.

Bantam Doubleday Dell Books for Young Readers: Cover illustration by Melodye Rosales from *Jackson Jones and the Puddle of Thorns* by Mary Quattlebaum. Illustration copyright © 1994 by Melodye Rosales.

Children's Better Health Institute, Benjamin Franklin Literary & Medical Society, Inc., Indianapolis, IN: "Kids and Kicks" by Deborah H. Deford from *U. S. Kids, A Weekly Reader Magazine*, October/November 1991. Text copyright © 1991 by Children's Better Health Institute.

Childrens Press, Inc.: From *Sleeping and Dreaming* by Rita Milios. Text copyright © 1987 by Regensteiner Publishing Enterprises, Inc.

Crown Publishers, Inc.: *Lester's Dog* by Karen Hesse, illustrated by Nancy Carpenter. Text copyright © 1993 by Karen Hesse; illustrations copyright (1993) by Nancy Carpenter. Untitled poem (Retitled: "When I Wake . . .") from *Voices of the Wild* by Jonathan London. Text copyright © 1993 by Jonathan London.

Dial Books for Young Readers, a division of Penguin Books USA Inc.: Cover illustration by Jerry Pinkney from *Tanya's Reunion* by Valerie Flournoy. Illustration copyright © 1995 by Jerry Pinkney. Illustrations by Jerry Pinkney from *The Patchwork Quilt* by Valerie Flournoy. Illustrations copyright © 1985 by Jerry Pinkney. Cover illustration by Jerry Pinkney from *John Henry* by Julius Lester. Illustration copyright © 1994 by Jerry Pinkney.

Dutton Children's Books, a division of Penguin Books USA Inc.: *Isla* by Arthur Dorros, illustrated by Elisa Kleven. Text copyright © 1995 by Arthur Dorros; illustrations copyright © 1995 by Elisa Kleven.

Farrar, Straus & Giroux, Inc.: Cover illustration from *Archibald Frisby* by Michael Chesworth. Copyright © 1994 by Michael Chesworth. *Brave Irene* by William Steig. Copyright © 1986 by William Steig.

Naomi F. Faust: "Black Parent to Child" (Retitled: "Parent to Child") from *All Beautiful Things* by Naomi F. Faust. Published by Lotus Press, Detroit, Michigan, distributed by Michigan State University Press.

Hampton-Brown Books: Cover illustration by Raphaelle Goethais from *A Chorus of Cultures* by Alma Flor Ada, Violet J. Harris, and Lee Bennett Hopkins. Copyright © 1993 by Hampton-Brown Books.

Harcourt Brace & Company: "After the Last Hard Freeze" from *In for Winter, Out for Spring* by Arnold Adoff, illustrated by Jerry Pinkney. Text copyright © 1991 by Arnold Adoff; illustrations copyright © 1991 by Jerry Pinkney. Cover photograph from *The Piñata Maker/El Piñatero* by George Ancona. Copyright © 1994 by George Ancona. From *The Science Book of Color* (Retitled: "What Is Color?") by Neil Ardley. Text copyright © 1991 by Neil Ardley. Cover illustration from *The Magic Fan* by Keith Baker. Illustration copyright © 1989 by Keith Baker. Cover illustration by Scott Medlock from *Extra Innings*, selected by Lee Bennett Hopkins. Illustration copyright © 1993 by Scott Medlock. Cover illustration from *Frida María: A Story of the Old Southwest* by Deborah Nourse Lattimore. Copyright © 1994 by Deborah Nourse Lattimore.

HarperCollins Publishers: Cover illustration by Ashley Bryan from *The Story of the Three Kingdoms* by Walter Dean Myers. Illustration copyright © 1995 by Ashley Bryan. *Storm in the Night* by Mary Stolz, illustrated by Pat Cummings. Text copyright © 1988 by Mary Stolz; illustrations copyright © 1988 by Pat Cummings.

Houghton Mifflin Company: Cover illustration by Blair Lent from *The Wave* by Margaret Hodges. Illustration copyright © 1964 by Blair Lent.

Hyperion Books for Children: Illustration by Steve Cieslawski from *At the Crack of the Bat: Baseball Poems*, compiled by Lillian Morrison. Illustration copyright © 1992 by Steve Cieslawski.

Little, Brown and Company: From *Centerfield Ballhawk* by Matt Christopher. Text copyright © 1992 by Matthew F. Christopher. Cover illustration by Peter Parnall from *Annie and the Old One* by Miska Miles. Illustration copyright © 1971 by Peter Parnall.

Lothrop, Lee & Shepard Books, a division of William Morrow & Company, Inc.: Cover illustration by Alan Tiegreen from *Ramona Quimby, Age 8* by Beverly Cleary. Copyright © 1981 by Beverly Cleary.

Macmillan Publishing Company: Cover illustration by Jerry Pinkney from *Turtle in July* by Marilyn Singer. Illustration copyright © 1989 by Jerry Pinkney.

Mike Makley: "The New Kid" by Mike Makley.

Morrow Junior Books, a division of William Morrow & Company, Inc.: Cover illustration by Alan Tiegreen from *Ramona the Brave* by Beverly Cleary. Copyright © 1975 by Beverly Cleary. *City Green* by DyAnne DiSalvo-Ryan. Copyright © 1994 by DyAnne DiSalvo-Ryan.

Northland Publishing, Flagstaff, AZ: *The Three Little Javelinas* by Susan Lowell, illustrated by Jim Harris. Text copyright © 1992 by Susan Lowell; illustrations copyright © 1992 by Jim Harris.

Philomel Books: *Appelemando's Dreams* by Patricia Polacco. Copyright © 1991 by Patricia Polacco. *Lon PoPo: A Red-Riding Hood Story from China* by Ed Young. Copyright © 1989 by Ed Young.

Plays, Inc.: "The Mystery of the Sounds in the Night" by Joan Lowery Nixon from *PLAYS: The Drama Magazine for Young People*, October 1990. Text copyright © 1990 by Plays, Inc. This play is for reading purposes only; for permission to produce, write to Plays, Inc., 120 Boylston Street, Boston, MA 02116.

Marian Reiner, on behalf of Isabel Joshlin Glaser: "Playing Outfield" by Isabel Joshlin Glaser. Text copyright © 1993 by Isabel Joshlin Glaser. "Prediction: School P. E." by Isabel Joshlin Glaser. Text copyright © 1990 by Isabel Joshlin Glaser.

Rizzoli International Publications, Inc., New York: Cover illustration by Du_an Petricic from *The Color of Things* by Vivienne Shalom. Illustration copyright © 1995 by Du_an Petricic.

Simon & Schuster Books for Young Readers, a division of Simon & Schuster: Cover illustration by Jerry Pinkney from *Half a Moon and One Whole Star* by Crescent Dragonwagon. Illustration copyright © 1986 by Jerry Pinkney. Cover illustration from *Up Goes the Skyscraper!* by Gail Gibbons. Copyright © 1986 by Gail Gibbons. Cover illustration by Floyd Cooper from *Papa Tells Chita a Story* by Elizabeth Fitzgerald Howard. Illustration copyright © 1995 by Floyd Cooper. Cover illustration by Marjorie Priceman from *Zin! Zin! Zin! A Violin* by Lloyd Moss. Illustration copyright © 1995 by Marjorie Priceman. Cover illustration from *Dinosaur Dream* by Dennis Nolan. Copyright © 1990 by Dennis Nolan.

Smithsonian Institution Press, Washington, DC: Untitled poem (Retitled: "A wolf . . .") from *Teton Sioux Music*, translated by Frances Densmore, in Bureau of American Ethnology, Bulletin #61.

Weekly Reader Corporation: "Think Positive!" from *Current Health® 1 Magazine*, April 1993. Text copyright © 1993 by Weekly Reader Corporation.

Nellie Wong: "How a Girl Got Her Chinese Name" from *Dreams in Harrison Railroad Park* by Nellie Wong. Published by Kelsey Street Press, 1977.

Wordsong, Boyds Mills Press, Inc.: Cover illustration by John Ward from *Families: Poems Celebrating the African American Experience*, selected by Dorothy S. Strickland and Michael R. Strickland. Illustration copyright © 1994 by John Ward.

Photo Credits

Key: (t) top, (b) bottom, (c) center, (l) left, (r) right, (i) inset, (bg) background.

Jonathan Kirn/Gamma Liaison, 2; Joe Devenney/The Image Bank, 3(bg); Maria Taglienti/The Image Bank, 3; Index Stock Photography, 42-43(bg), 44-45(bg); Andy Cox/Tony Stone Images, 44(b/l); David De Lossy/The Image Bank, 44(b/r), 50-51, 51(b/l); Steve Cavalier/Picture Perfect USA, 44-45; Superstock, 45(t), 259(t/r), 260-261(bg), 91(singer), 91(butterfly); Maltaverne/Picture Perfect USA, 45(b); Haraldo de Farla Castro/FPG International, 46(b); Craig Tuttle/The Stock Market, 46-47(bg)t, 50-51(bg); David W. Hamilton/The Image Bank, 46-47; Tom Tracy/Tony Stone Images, 47(t); Roy Gumpel/Gamma Liaison, 47(c); Tom Stewart/The Stock Market, 47(b); Philippe Plailly/Science Photo Library/Photo Researchers, 49; Bryan F. Peterson/The Stock Market, 50(t), 90(baseball); Dennis Berry/Stock Boston, 50(b); The Bettmann Archive, 52, 55; Icon Comm/FPG International, 52-53(bg); Blumebild/FPG International, 53; Grant V. Faint/The Image Bank, 54-55(bg); Blumebild/FPG International, 53; Grant V. Faint/The Image Bank, 54-55(bg); The Bettmann Archive, 55; John Lei/OPC; 60, 90(flashlight/glasses), 91(glasses), 92(paper, pens, scissors), 93(bowls), 98, 100-101, 102, 107, 114, 232-233, 288; Harcourt Brace & Company, 82-83, 103, 258; C. Middlebrook/Picture Perfect USA, 88-89(pencils); Stuart Frawley/Picture Perfect USA, 88(white light); James Randkiev/Tony Stone Images, 88-89(grass); Uniphoto, 88(rose); Stuart Westmorland/Tony Stone Images, 89(fish); P&M Walton/Picture Perfect USA, 89(rainbow); Aitch/Picture Perfect USA, 89(CD); SP Productions/Picture Perfect USA, 90-91(sunset); Otto Rogge/The Stock market, 90-91(geese); B. F. Peterson/WestStock, 91(parrot); Tim Davis/Tony Stone Images, 92(frog); Renee Lynn/Tony Stone Images, 92(leaf); Comstock, 93(paint cans), 93(paint motif); Wally Emerson, 94-95; Courtesy of Jerry Pinkney, 99, 102(t), 106; Antonio Rosario/The Image Bank, 104-105(bg); Chuck Savage/The Stock Market, 104-105(i); (clockwise from top) Charles Thatcher/Tony Stone Images; Gary S. Chapman/The Image Bank; Bruce Ayres/Tony Stone Images; Jay Freis/The Image Bank; Ed Wheeler/The Stock Market; Michael Melford/The Image Bank; Charles Thatcher/Tony Stone Images; Melchior DelGiacomo/The Image Bank; Wenberg-Clark/The Image Bank; Co Rentmeester/The Image Bank; Jon Feingar/The Stock Market; Alan Levenson/Tony Stone Images; David W. Hamilton/The Image Bank; Bruce Ayres/Tony Stone Images; Kay Chernush/The Image Bank; David W. Hamilton/The Image Bank; Walter Bibikow/The Image Bank; Gary Gladstone/The Image Bank, 104-105; Courtesy of Jerry Pinkney, 106; Tony Stone Images, 159; Dale Higgins/Harcourt Brace & Company, 230; Sal DiMarco/Black Star/Harcourt Brace & Company, 255; Matt Bradley, 259(t/l), 259(c), 259(b), 260-261; Nancy Pierce/Black Star/Harcourt Brace & Company, 275(l); Courtesy of Matt Christopher, 275(r); Tom Sobolik/Black Star/Harcourt Brace & Company, 309; Ross Humphreys, 328; Davis Photography, 329

Illustration Credits

Guy Porfirio, Cover art

Theme 1: Wayne Vincent, 6-7, 13-17, 108
Theme 2: Doug Bowles, 8-9, 110-113, 236
Theme 3: Jeanne Berg, 10-13, 237, 238-241, 333

Nancy Carpenter, 1-2, 178-209; Leslie Wu, 1,2,6,10,14; Liz Callen, title page, 2,10-11,13,17; Elisa Kleven, 18-39; Richard McNeel, 52-54; Particia Polacco, 60-87; Diane Blasius, 93; Jerry Pinkney, 96-103, 106-107, 284-285; David Flaherty, 99; William Steig, 114-133; Liz Callen, 114-131; Pat Cummings, 134-161; Cameron Wasson, 162-164, 167, 170-171; Jim Clapp, 172-173; David Diaz, 174-175; Jose Cruz, 212-215; Leslie Wu, 216-231, 234-235; DyAnne DiSalvo-Ryan, 242-257; Obadinah Heavner, 258-261; Steve Cieslawski, 276-277; Lisa Pomerantz, 264-275, 278-279; Holly Cooper, 280-283; Ed Young, 288-311; Jim Harris, 312-331